W9-AKT-934

"This is a handy book with helpful answers for busy people."
—**Dr. Norman Geisler,** President of Southern Evangelical Seminary, and author of more than sixty books including *The Baker Encyclopedia of Apologetics*

"Charlie is a man of integrity, a true Berean, and a personal encouragement to me. I'm excited to see what the Lord has in store for this man of faith."
—**Jeremy Camp,** BEC Recording Artist and 2004 Dove Award winner

"I hope many seekers will give serious consideration to the thoughts so well expressed in this timely and pithy book. Well worth reading."
—**Charles Colson,** Founder of Prison Fellowship, author of more than twenty books, international speaker, radio commentator

"A refreshing model of 'conversational apologetics!' This book will equip you to be 'always ready to give an answer for the hope that lies within you.'"
—**Nancy Leigh DeMoss,** Author, Revive Our Hearts radio host

"The Christian faith is the most reasonable faith in the world, and Charlie Campbell shows that in a straightforward and down-to-earth way in this book. I thoroughly enjoyed reading it and plan to give it away to as many people as I can."
—**Brian Brodersen,** Associate Pastor, Calvary Chapel Costa Mesa, California

"I would like to both thank and congratulate Charlie on his *One Minute Answers To Skeptics Top Forty Questions.* It is both basic and excellent in that the answers are simple, accurate and precise to many questions that people have in their struggles to understand the Bible. I appreciated Charlie's ability to take the often difficult questions and answer very well."
—**Don McClure,** Pastor of Calvary Laguna, California

"*One Minute Answers* is a much needed book in the world today. Charlie Campbell has done an excellent job bringing to the reader answers to age-old questions. Charlie Campbell in, *One Minute Answers,* has shed light in a dark world. He's made it easy and enjoyable reading."
—**Mike MacIntosh,** Founder and President, Horizon International Ministries

"In his book, Charlie Campbell invites every honest skeptic to take a good look at the Christian worldview, if for no other reason than to be better informed as to how the Bible answers man's most intriguing and challenging questions and why Christianity is a reasonable faith. Succinctly written, *One Minute Answers to Skeptics' Top Forty Questions,* offers concise information for both skeptic and believer alike."
—**Jack Hibbs,** Pastor of Calvary Chapel Chino Hills, California

"I have heard that one definition of genius is taking things complex and being able to simplify them. I was impressed that such difficult questions could be adequately answered in such a few lines. I think the majority of Christians, who want and need answers to tough questions like these, often want a simple, sufficient answer without having to read an entire book on the subject. In quick, simple answers Charlie has done it. I know this was not easy, but on behalf of Christians everywhere in all sincerity, thanks."
—**Bryan Newberry,** Pastor of Calvary Chapel San Diego, California

"Succinctly and very powerfully answers skeptics' questions...It is immensely readable....I highly recommend this book."
—**William M. Alnor, Ph.D.,** Author, Professor (California State University, East Bay); Access Director, The Spiritual Counterfeits Project, Berkeley, California

"Great primer for apologetics! *One Minute Answers* strikes a great balance–crisp, well-structured responses that also whet the appetite for deeper study. Seekers, skeptics, and believers will all benefit from Charlie's clear presentation and readable style."
–**Lloyd Pulley,** Pastor of Calvary Chapel Old Bridge, New Jersey

"Charlie Campbell has done a wonderful job of earnestly contending for the faith. His depth of thought will be a powerful tool for leaders and defenders of the faith and his succinct clarity will be a blessing to all who want to know the truth."
—**Britt Merrick,** Senior Pastor at Reality Carpinteria, California

"Charlie Campbell provides believers with one of the most useful tools to come along in a long time. In fact, I know of no other book that covers so much important territory in such a short time."
—**George Bryson,** Author, Missionary

"It is with tremendous excitement that I can wholeheartedly recommend this long anticipated work by Charlie Campbell."
—**Chuck Wooley,** Pastor of The Bridge Calvary Chapel, Palm Springs, California

"Charlie Campbell has an incredible gift for simplifying that which can seem complicated. This book is a great example of that."
—**Rob Salvato,** Pastor of Calvary Chapel Vista, California

"A simple answer that you can remember is more useful than a complex answer that you can't quite recall. *One Minute Answers* provides answers you can give when on the spot."
—**Carl Westerlund,** Director of The School of Ministry at Calvary Chapel Costa Mesa, California

ONE MINUTE
ANSWERS
to SKEPTICS'
TOP FORTY QUESTIONS

AQUINTAS
PUBLISHING

ONE MINUTE
ANSWERS
to SKEPTICS'
TOP FORTY QUESTIONS

CHARLIE H. CAMPBELL

AQUINTAS
Publishing

ONE MINUTE ANSWERS TO SKEPTICS' TOP FORTY QUESTIONS

Additional copies of this book may be purchased at AlwaysBeReady.com

Published by Aquintas Publishing, USA
ISBN: 1-59751-999-5

Printed in the United States of America.
Fourth Printing: September, 2006

DEDICATION

This book is dedicated to high school and college age people who are questioning the validity of the Christian faith,[1] as well as to all those who desire to give a defense of the Christian faith to those who ask (1 Peter 3:15).

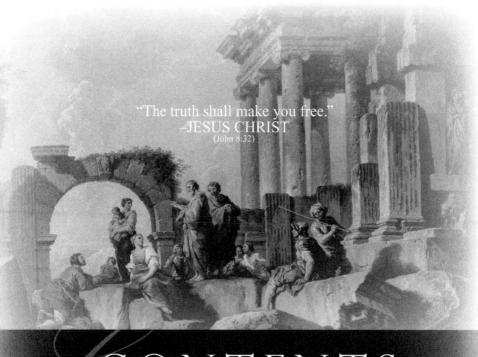

"The truth shall make you free."
–JESUS CHRIST
(John 8:32)

CONTENTS

1. "What evidence do you have that there is a God?"

2. "What evidence do you have that the Bible is actually true?"

3. "Hasn't the Bible undergone corruption as it was translated hundreds of times down through the centuries?"

4. "What about those who have never heard of Jesus? Will they be condemned to hell?"

5. "If God is so loving, why does He allow evil and suffering?"

6. "How do you know if Jesus even existed?"

7. "How can you say that Jesus is the only way to heaven?"

8. "Wasn't the deity of Christ an invention by the church during the fourth century at the Council of Nicea?"

9. "Doesn't it seem unfair and narrow that God would only save people through Jesus?"

10. "How can a loving God send somebody to hell?"

11. "Haven't certain books of the Bible been lost?"

12. "Isn't there a conflict between the God in the Old Testament, who is often portrayed as cruel, and the God of the New Testament who seems very loving?"

13. "Why do Christians reject the apocryphal writings that are in the Catholic Bible?"

14. "Doesn't the Bible have a bunch of contradictions in it?"

15. "Wasn't the New Testament written down hundreds of years *after* Jesus lived? Wouldn't that make it unreliable?"

16. "Doesn't the Bible have scientific errors in it?"

17. "How do you know that Christianity is true and not some other religion like Buddhism or Islam?"

18. "What about homosexuals? Do you believe that they go to hell?"

19. "How do you know that Jesus rose from the dead?"

20. "What about evolution? Haven't Darwin's theories disproved God's existence?"

21. "If everything needs a maker, as Christians seem to suggest, then who made God?"

22. "Well, if God doesn't need a maker [see previous question and answer], why couldn't we just say that the universe doesn't need a maker either?"

23. "Can God make a rock so big that He cannot move it? Yes or No?"

24. "How (or where) did Cain get his wife?"

25. "How can you adhere to a religion that would advocate such events as the Crusades?"

26. "What about the Old Testament, when Joshua and the nation of Israel were commanded by God to go through the land of Canaan and destroy everyone? How can you believe in a God who would command such a thing?"

27. "Do you think that it's right to try and force your beliefs upon other people?"

28. "Where did the dinosaurs come from? Didn't dinosaurs live millions of years before man?"

29. "Why aren't dinosaurs mentioned in the Bible?"

30. "How could dinosaurs fit on Noah's ark? If dinosaurs *were* on Noah's ark, why aren't they around today?"

31. "How could all the races, with their different skin colors, come from Noah's family?"

32. "Don't all religions basically teach the same thing?"

33. "Don't Christians worship the same God as Muslims?"

34. "What makes you think that the Qur'an is not divinely inspired?"

35. "What makes you think that the Book of Mormon is not trustworthy?"

36. "If Christianity is true, why can't the different denominations agree on what to believe?"

37. "Aren't there a bunch of hypocrites in the church?"

38. "Does it really matter *what* a person believes as long as they are sincere?"

39. "How could I ever be happy in heaven, knowing that my loved ones are in hell?"

40. "Isn't being a good person enough to get to heaven?"

ACKNOWLEDGMENTS

I am indebted to the following men for their scholarly research and writings that have shaped my thinking, strengthened my faith, and inspired me with ways to answer the kinds of questions I address in this book: Dr. Norman Geisler, Dr. William Lane Craig, Dr. Ravi Zacharias, Dr. J. P. Moreland, Ron Rhodes, Greg Koukl, Dr. Josh McDowell, Dr. Phillip E. Johnson, Dr. Francis Beckwith, Dr. John Ankerberg, Lee Strobel, Dr. Michael Behe, Dr. Jonathan Wells, Dr. Charles Colson, Dr. John Walvoord, Dr. Henry Morris, Dr. Gary Habermas, Dave Hunt, Don Stewart, Dr. Paul Copan, Dr. Ken Ham, Ron Carlson, Ray Comfort, Dan Story and C. S. Lewis.

Thank you Karen Robbins, Ron and Cindy Barger, Maryanne Hommel and Steve Erenyi for the hours you spent editing the manuscript of this book and for your invaluable suggestions.

Thank you Calvary Chapel Vista and especially Rob Nash for your encouragement, love and prayers.

Thank you Anastasia, Selah, Addison and Caden, my wonderful family, for your undying, amazing love and support. You are my greatest treasures.

My deepest gratitude is reserved for You Jesus, my Friend, Shepherd, Savior and King. Thank You for rescuing me from my unbelief and sin in 1990. It is a joy, too deep for words, to know You and serve You. It is for You that I live and breathe.

$\mathscr{A}$RE YOU A SKEPTIC?

Do you have questions or doubts about the existence of God? Do you wonder if what the Bible says is really true? Do you question why God would allow evil and suffering? If so, I can relate. Those are the kinds of questions I used to have. Although I was raised in a Christian home, the faith I had as a child eroded into agnosticism and eventually atheism some time after junior high school. It was not until 1990, when I received intellectually satisfying answers to my questions, that my faith in God was slowly resurrected.

Skepticism regarding matters of the Christian faith is, of course, nothing new. The Bible itself mentions many people who were skeptics or who had questions and doubts about such matters. The people in Capernaum, on the shore of the Sea of Galilee, wanted to have evidence *before* they would believe. They asked Jesus:

> "What sign will You perform then, that we may see it and believe You? What work will You do?" (John 6:30)

The imprisoned, and apparently doubting, John the Baptist, whose faith had at one time been so strong, sent two messengers to ask Jesus:

> "Are You the Coming One, or do we look for another?" (Luke 7:19)

Thomas, one of the original twelve disciples, was skeptical of Jesus' resurrection, and said:

> "Unless I see in His hands the print of the nails, and put my finger into the print of the nails, and put my hand into His side, I will not believe." (John 20:25)

Pontius Pilate questioned Jesus about who He was and then finally asked:

> "What is truth?" (John 18:38)

We could add to this list the two disciples leaving Jerusalem after Jesus' crucifixion (Luke 24:13) and others.

How did Jesus respond to these people who had honest doubts and questions? Did He condemn them? Did He exhort them to put away their questions, suppress their doubts, and simply believe? No. Jesus, lovingly and graciously, gave them answers. He gave them evidence.

To John the Baptist, Jesus sent two messengers to tell of all the miraculous things He had just done (Luke 7:21-23). To doubting Thomas, Jesus showed Himself alive, after His crucifixion, and allowed Thomas to see the wounds in His hands and His side (John 20:26-29). For the discouraged disciples leaving Jerusalem convinced that Jesus' death disproved any claim He had to be the Messiah, Jesus met them, after His resurrection, and showed them how the Scriptures had prophesied long beforehand that the Messiah was going to suffer (Luke 24:13-27). The Bible tells us that Jesus gave "many convincing *proofs*" (Acts 1:3, NASB).

The God of the Bible does not require that we blindly follow Him. For example:

- The Bible tells us to "*examine* everything *carefully*" and to only believe that which is actually true (1 Thessalonians 5:21, Colossians 2:4)

- The Bible commends the people in the city of Berea for *verifying* that the words spoken by the apostle Paul were actually true (Acts 17:11)

- God desires that we use our *minds*, not just our hearts (Matthew 22:37)

- God says, "Come now, and let us *reason* together" (Isaiah 1:18)

- The Bible exhorts Christians to have *answers* for people with questions (1 Peter 3:15)

- God desires all people "to come to the *knowledge* of the *truth*" (1 Timothy 2:4)

Why does God want to reason with you? Why does He want you to come to the knowledge of the truth? Why does He want Christians to have answers for you? He loves you and wants to have a relationship with you (John 3:16). He wants you to experience the joy and wonder of knowing Him and His Son, Jesus Christ, not only in this life, but in eternity.

Have your unanswered questions regarding Christianity kept you from knowing God? My hope and prayer for you is that this book will help answer your questions. Ultimately, my prayer is that you will come to realize and know, experientially, the joy of having a relationship with Jesus. He truly is the Son of God. He came to this earth two thousand years ago, died on the cross for your sins, and rose again so that you might experience God's forgiveness and everlasting life.

If the short answers in this book do not sufficiently lay to rest your doubts, I urge you to pick up one of the following books:

- *Reasonable Faith: Christian Truth and Apologetics*
  by Dr. William Lane Craig

- *I Don't Have Enough Faith To Be An Atheist*
  by Dr. Norman Geisler and Frank Turek

- *Scaling the Secular City*
  by Dr. J. P. Moreland

- *The Case For Faith*
  by Lee Strobel

These books, and the others I mention in the endnotes, deal with many of the issues addressed in this book in an in-depth manner. If you desire to know God in a personal way, please see "Steps to Peace With God" on page 107.

May God bless you and guide you into the truth.

ℐNTRODUCTION

I was eating lunch at a restaurant with a friend a while back when our waitress saw our opened Bibles on the table. I am always amazed at the conversations that ensue after someone sees an open Bible. Doing a double-take at the open Bibles, she asked, "Are you guys Christians or something?" We told her, "Yes," and asked her if she had any spiritual beliefs.[2] She said that she *used to be* a Christian, but had changed her views a few years ago while she was taking a philosophy class at a local college. She went on to tell us that she now believed all roads lead to heaven. We talked with her for a moment about Jesus' exclusive claims regarding salvation in John 14:6 ("I am the way, the truth, and the life. No one comes to the Father except through Me") and the fact that He proved that what He was saying was true by His resurrection from the dead. She listened intently and then had to get back to work.

As ambassadors for Christ (2 Corinthians 5:20) we need to be prepared (1 Peter 3:15, Jude 3) for open doors to speak of Christ and share the truth. The doors are often only open for a minute and then they are shut.

What follows in this book are examples of ways you can answer a variety of questions in under a minute. When someone asks me, "What evidence do you have that the Bible is actually true?" I do not attempt to walk them through a whole pile of evidence ("The *eighth* reason is..."). I try to answer their question in under a minute or two. Frankly, that is all the time people often have before their cell phone rings, the baby starts crying, or they have to get back to work. If they want to hear a more in-depth response to their question, I let them know that I would be glad to go on.

The questions compiled herein, in no particular order, are forty of the most common questions unbelievers and skeptics pose to Christians about God, the Bible, hell, salvation, and so on. I do not mean to imply by the title of the book that these are the most challenging or difficult questions that skeptics *could* ask, only that these are, in my opinion, forty of the most popular questions they *do* ask.

My prayer for you, if you are already a Christian,

is that your faith will be strengthened and you will be better equipped to answer these questions the next time they come up in your own life.

May God bless this book for His glory, the strengthening of the saints and the furtherance of the gospel.

Charlie H. Campbell
September 2005

ON THE UNIVERSE:

"A proponent of the big bang theory, at least if he is an atheist, must believe that the matter of the universe came from nothing and by nothing."

–Anthony Kenny, D.Phil., D.Litt. (1931-), former Pro-Vice-Chancellor of the University of Oxford (1984-2002), President of the British Academy (1989-1993), and author of more than forty books on philosophy and history; *The Five Ways: St. Thomas Aquinas' Proofs of God's Existence,* 1969, p. 66.

"When you realize that the laws of nature must be incredibly finely tuned to produce the universe we see, that conspires to plant the idea that the universe did not just happen, but that there must be a purpose behind it."

–John Polkinghorne, Ph.D. (1930-), author, former physicist and Professor of Theoretical Physics at Cambridge University, 2002 winner of the Templeton Prize. "Science Finds God," *Newsweek,* July 20, 1998.

26

1 "What evidence do you have that there is a God?"

The very existence of the universe itself is evidence that there is a God. Let's think about this for a moment. There are only three options for the existence of the universe. One, that it has always been. Two, that it came into being by itself. Three, that it was created. The first option, that the universe is eternal, has been utterly rejected by the scientific community. The motion of the galaxies, the background radiation echo, and other evidences all overwhelmingly point to the fact that the universe sprang into existence at a particular point in time, something scientists call the Big Bang. Option two, that the universe created itself, is philosophically impossible. Of course, before the universe existed it would not have been around to do the creating. Obviously, a non-existent universe could not have done anything! It did not exist. We all know that nothing can not do anything. Nothing is *no*thing. It (if we could even call nothing an *it!*) cannot see, smell, act, think, or create. So option one and two can be thrown out on scientific and philosophical grounds. Option three, that something or someone outside of the universe created the universe, is the only reasonable option.

Let's imagine I am holding up a painting. When you see a painting, what proof do you need to establish the fact that a painter exists? Nothing else besides the painting itself. The painting is absolute proof that there was a painter. You do not need to see the painter to believe that he or she exists. The painting is all the evidence you need. It would not be there if the painter did not exist, and so it is with the universe. The existence of the universe itself proves absolutely that there is a creator.[3]

ON ATHEISM:

"I am persuaded that men think there is no God because they wish there were none. They find it hard to believe in God, and to go on in sin, so they try to get an easy conscience by denying His existence."
–**Charles H. Spurgeon** (1834-1892), British preacher.

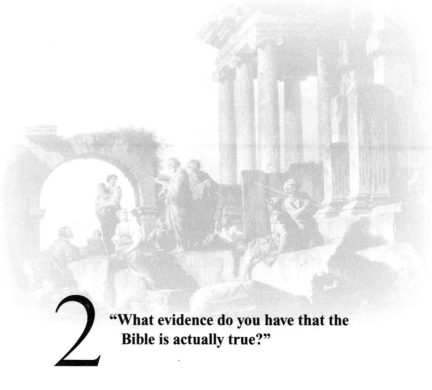

2 "What evidence do you have that the Bible is actually true?"

If I had to narrow it down to a few evidences, I would probably say: *fulfilled prophecies, archaeological discoveries*, and the Bible's amazing *unity*.

The Bible, unlike any other religious book, has demonstrated itself to be the Word of God through its ability to rightly predict the future. There are literally hundreds of very specific prophecies in the Bible that were spoken hundreds of years before their fulfillment that have already come to pass.[4] No other religious book can verify itself in this way.

The Bible has also been proven to be historically reliable by numerous archaeological discoveries. To date, there have been more than 25,000 archaeological discoveries that have verified the names of persons, places, events, and customs mentioned in the Bible.

Finally, there is the Bible's amazing unity. Here is a book that is actually a collection of sixty-six different books, written down by more than forty different authors, over a period of 1,500 plus years, on three different continents, in three different languages, and it addresses life's most controversial topics from beginning to end. You would think there would be chaos, confusion, and contradictions, yet the Bible miraculously remains absolutely consistent and internally harmonious from beginning to end.[5] These three evidences (fulfilled prophecy, archaeological discoveries, and the Bible's amazing unity) build a compelling case for the divine origin and historical reliability of the Bible.[6]

ON ARCHAEOLOGY:

"Archaeological work has unquestionably strengthened confidence in the reliability of the Scriptural record. More than one archaeologist has found his respect for the Bible increased by the experience of excavation in Palestine."

–Millar Burrows, Ph.D. (1889-1980), Yale University Professor; *What Mean These Stones?*, 1941, p. 1.

3 "Hasn't the Bible undergone corruption as it was translated hundreds of times down through the centuries?"

The Bible *has* been translated into hundreds of different languages down through the centuries. You are right about that, but the text of the Bible has been accurately preserved all the way through. How do we know that to be the case?

First, there is the *manuscript evidence*. Today, there exists several thousand partial and complete, ancient handwritten manuscript copies of the Bible, some dating as far back as the third century B.C.[7] These manuscripts have allowed textual critics and scholars to verify that the Bible we have today is the same Bible the early church had.

Secondly, there are the *writings of the church fathers*. By church fathers, I am referring to leaders in the early church.[8] In their commentaries on the Bible, their letters to one another, and their letters to other churches, these men quoted the New Testament Scriptures alone more than 86,000 times. Their quotations have allowed scholars to reconstruct 99.86% of the New Testament. There are only eleven verses in the New Testament that the church fathers apparently never cited.

These two evidences, the manuscript evidence and the writings of the church fathers, verify conclusively that the original text of the Bible has been accurately preserved.[9]

ON THE BIBLE:

"...the last foundation for any doubt that the Scriptures have come down to us substantially as they were written has now been removed. Both the authenticity and the general integrity of the books of the New Testament may be regarded as finally established."

–**Sir Frederic Kenyon** (1863-1952), former director and principal librarian of the British Museum, and one of the leading authorities on the reliability of ancient manuscripts; *The Bible and Archaeology*, 1940, pp. 288-289.

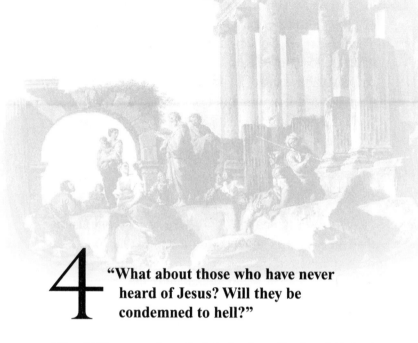

4

"What about those who have never heard of Jesus? Will they be condemned to hell?"

The Bible says that God is loving (Psalm 103:8, 1 John 4:10) and that He is not willing that any should perish (2 Peter 3:9). If a person has never heard of Jesus, the Bible says that God is going to be absolutely fair with them (Psalm 98:9), and that He will judge them based on what they do know through the testimony of creation and their conscience (Romans 1:20, 2:12-15).

If a person truly seeks to know God, the Bible says that "God is a rewarder of those who diligently seek Him (Hebrews 11:6)." There are many ways that God can get the truth about salvation to those who truly seek to know Him. He can send a missionary (Acts 10),[10] a radio broadcast, or a Bible (Psalm 119:130). Theoretically God could send a vision (Daniel 2) or an angel (Revelation 14:6).[11] You *have* heard the truth. You have heard of Jesus' death on the cross for your sins and God will hold you accountable for what you do with that information.[12]

ON SCIENCE:

"It was my science that drove me to the conclusion that the world is much more complicated than can be explained by science, it is only through the supernatural that I can understand the mystery of existence."

–Allan Sandage, Ph.D. (1926-), American Astronomer, winner of the Helen B. Warner Prize for Astronomy in 1957, the Gold Medal of the Royal Astronomical Society in 1967, the Henry Norris Russell Lectureship in 1972 and the Bruce Medal in 1975. *Science Finds God*, Newsweek, July 20, 1998.

"Many have a feeling that somehow intelligence must have been involved in the laws of the universe....I strongly sense the presence and actions of a creative being far beyond myself and yet always personal and close by."

–Charles Townes, Ph.D. (1915-), physicist, author, Professor in the Graduate School at the University of California at Berkeley, shared the 1964 Nobel Prize in Physics for inventing the laser, holds honorary degrees from more than 25 universities. "Science Finds God," *Newsweek*, July 20, 1998.

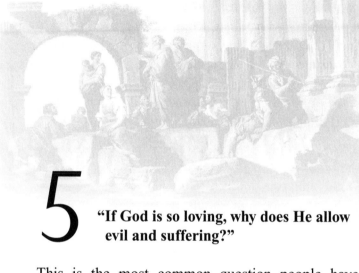

5 "If God is so loving, why does He allow evil and suffering?"

This is the most common question people have regarding God. Here is an interesting question for *you* to consider. What do you propose God should do about it? To stop evil and suffering, God would have to stop every act that causes any suffering. To do that, He would have to stop those who cause the suffering (adulterers, liars, murderers, criminals, fornicators, etc.). Wouldn't that mean He would have to put a stop to you too? Haven't you, by your own actions, caused some of the suffering that exists in the world? Haven't you hurt somebody's feelings? My friend, God has not destroyed evil because He would have to destroy us. By permitting evil and suffering to continue, God is actually showing the world *mercy*.

The Bible says that there *is* coming a day when God will stop evil (2 Peter 3:7-13). He will judge sinners, put them away forever, and create a new heaven and a new earth where there will no longer be any death, mourning, crying, or pain (Revelation 21:4). In the meantime, God is using the suffering that exists for good (Romans 8:28, Philippians 1:12). Often, when a person is suffering, they turn to God and receive the kind of help they truly need.

ON SUFFERING:

"God whispers to us in our pleasures, speaks in our conscience, but shouts in our pains: it is His megaphone to rouse a deaf world."

–C. S. Lewis (1898-1963), Professor of Medieval and Renaissance Literature at the University of Cambridge; *The Problem of Pain*, 1962, p. 93.

"Supposing you eliminated suffering, what a dreadful place the world would be! I would almost rather eliminate happiness. The world would be the most ghastly place because everything that corrects the tendency of this unspeakable little creature, man, to feel over-important and over-pleased with himself would disappear. He's bad enough now, but he would be absolutely intolerable if he never suffered."

–Malcolm Muggeridge (1903-1990), British author and journalist, educated at Cambridge University, high-profile agnostic for most of his life until he converted to Christianity sometime between 1966 and 1969; *Jesus Rediscovered*, 1969, pp. 199-200.

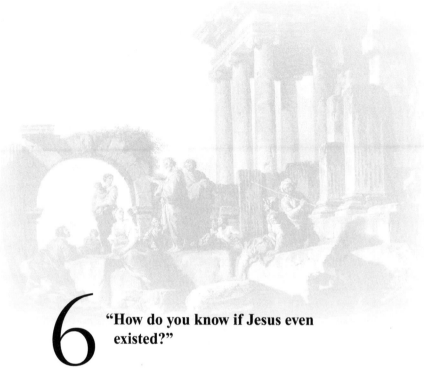

6 "How do you know if Jesus even existed?"

Of course the New Testament, which has proven to be a reliable historical record, attests to His life. On top of that, there are at least thirty-nine sources *outside* of the Bible that attest to more than a hundred facts regarding Jesus' life, teachings, crucifixion, and resurrection.[13] Take, for example, Flavius Josephus, a first century Roman historian. He affirms, not only that Jesus lived, but that He was "a doer of amazing deeds," that "Pilate condemned Him to be crucified to die," that He was a teacher who "won over many Jews and many of the Greeks" and that He was reportedly seen alive by His disciples after His crucifixion.[14] A second extrabiblical source would be the Babylonian Talmud. This collection of ancient Jewish writings mentions Jesus, even saying that He was killed on the eve of Passover,[15] just as the Biblical account describes.[16] The evidence is certain. Jesus of Nazareth was a real person.[17]

ON JESUS:

"At this time there was a wise man who was called Jesus. And his conduct was good, and he was known to be virtuous. And many people from among the Jews and the other nations became his disciples. Pilate condemned Him to be crucified to die. And those who had become his disciples did not abandon his discipleship. They reported that He had appeared to them three days after his crucifixion and that He was alive."

–**Flavius Josephus** (A.D. 37-c.100), first century Roman historian; *The Antiquities of the Jews*, 18:3.

"He was the greatest human being who has ever lived. He was a moral genius. His ethical sense was unique. He was the intrinsically wisest person that I've ever encountered in my life or in my reading. His commitment was total and led to his own death, much to the detriment of the world..."

–**Charles Templeton** (1915-2001), atheist, author, in interview with Lee Strobel; *The Case for Faith*, 2000, p. 17.

7 "How can you say that Jesus is the only way to heaven?"

That is what the Bible teaches.[18] Let's imagine for a moment that you have just hurt my feelings in a terrible way. You said and did some really mean things to me. Would you be able to go to just anyone and apologize to them in order to make right *our* relationship? Of course not. The same is true in our relationship with God. Mankind has sinned against God by the things we have said and done.[19] Therefore, we must go back to Him in order to have our relationship restored, not Buddha, Allah, Krishna, or some other imaginary, man-made deity. A person must go to, and through Jesus, because He *is* God. He is not a city, like Rome, of which it might be said, "All roads lead to Rome." God is a personal being who has provided the free gift of salvation (Romans 6:23) to all who will put their trust in His Son, Jesus. If a person puts his faith in another savior (Buddha, Brahman, Allah), they will find on judgment day that their god has done nothing for their eternal well-being, because their "so-called god" (1 Corinthians 8:5) does not exist (Isaiah 43:11, 45:5).

ON GOD:

"To look out at this kind of creation and not believe in God is to me impossible."
–John Glenn, Ph.D. (1921-), astronaut. Words spoken as he looked out of the Space Shuttle *Discovery*, November 4, 1998. "Astronauts Who Found God," by Chuck Colson, BreakPoint, November 5, 1998.

"God's nature is revealed most perfectly in the life and teachings of Jesus of Nazareth, as recorded in the New Testament of the Bible, who was sent by God to reveal the divine nature."
–George F. R. Ellis, Ph.D. (1939-), leading theoretical cosmologist, educated at Cambridge University, Professor of Applied Mathematics at the University of Cape Town, South Africa, recipient of the Templeton Prize (2004) and the author of numerous books. Quote above taken from *Quantum Cosmology and the Laws of Nature*, 1997, edited by Nancey Murphy and others, cited in "Stephen Hawking, the Big Bang, and God," by Dr. Henry F. Schaefer, III.

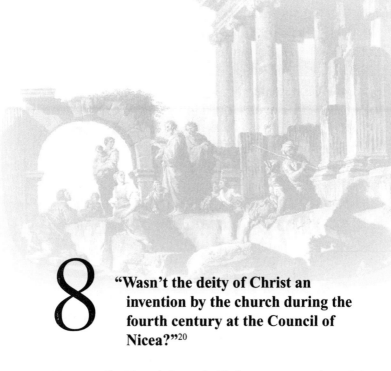

8

"Wasn't the deity of Christ an invention by the church during the fourth century at the Council of Nicea?"[20]

Not at all. The deity of Christ was mentioned in the Old Testament era more than 600 years before Jesus was born. Isaiah, the prophet, foretold that the Messiah would be called "Mighty *God*" in Isaiah 9:6. That certainly proved true.

The New Testament, which was completed in the first century, long before the Council of Nicea, is full of affirmations of Christ's deity.[21] For instance, Thomas called Jesus, "My Lord and my God!" (John 20:28). Paul calls Jesus, "our great God and Savior Jesus Christ" (Titus 2:13). John called Jesus "God" in the opening verse of his Gospel (John 1:1). Jesus took the name of God used in the Old Testament, "I AM," (Exodus 3:14) and applied it to Himself in John 8:58. He also said that God was His Father, resulting in some of His listeners trying to stone Him for making Himself "equal with God" (John 5:18, 10:33).

The second century writings of church fathers, like Ignatius, Polycarp, Justin Martyr, Irenaeus and Clement of Alexandria, also contain many references to Christ's deity.[22]

The resolution passed at the Council of Nicea in the fourth century (A.D. 325) was only a reaffirmation of what the church at large already believed.

ON JESUS:

"A man who was merely a man and said the sort of things Jesus said would not be a great moral teacher. He would either be a lunatic–on the level with the man who says he is a poached egg–or else he would be the Devil of Hell. You must make your choice. Either this man was, and is, the Son of God: or else a madman or something worse. You can shut Him up for a fool, you can spit at Him and kill Him as a demon; or you can fall at His feet and call Him Lord and God. But let us not come with any patronizing nonsense about His being a great human teacher. He has not left that open to us. He did not intend to."

–**C. S. Lewis** (1898-1963), Professor of Medieval and Renaissance Literature at the University of Cambridge; *Mere Christianity*, 1960, pp. 40-41.

9

"Doesn't it seem unfair and narrow that God would only save people through Jesus?"

I do not see it that way. I think the question we should be asking is, "Why would God seek to save us at all?" When I consider my own sinfulness and the rampant rebellion and sinfulness that exists in the world today, I find it absolutely amazing that God has offered to save us at all!

Far from being a narrow, unfair offer of salvation, the Bible portrays God's offer of salvation as very gracious and broad. The Bible says that God loves the *whole* world (John 3:16, Romans 5:8), that Jesus died for the sins of *all* mankind (1 John 2:2) and that God is making salvation available to people on every continent. The gospel message is not just for Americans or Europeans, or some other people group. Jesus told His disciples to take the good news "even to the remotest part of the earth" (Acts 1:8, NASB). The Book of Revelation tells us that in heaven there will be people "from *every* nation and *all* tribes and peoples and tongues" (Revelation 7:9, NASB). God's offer of salvation is broad and gracious.

ON THE RESURRECTION:

"If Jesus remained dead, how can you explain the reality of the Christian church and its phenomenal growth in the first three centuries of the Christian era? Christ's church covered the Western world by the fourth century. A religious movement built on a lie could not have accomplished that....All the power of Rome and of the religious establishment in Jerusalem was geared to stop the Christian faith. All they had to do was to dig up the grave and to present the corpse. They didn't."

–Henry Schaefer III, Ph.D. (1944-), former professor of chemistry at the University of California, Berkeley, currently the Graham Perdue Professor of Chemistry at the University of Georgia. He has been nominated for the Nobel Prize and was recently cited as the third most quoted chemist in the world; Quote taken from his lecture, "Questions Intellectuals Ask About Christianity." See www.leaderu.com/offices/schaefer/docs/questions.html.

10 "How can a loving God send somebody to hell?"

The last thing God wants is for a person to end up in hell. The Bible says that God is "not willing that any should perish" (2 Peter 3:9) and that He "desires *all* men to be saved and to come to the knowledge of the truth" (1 Timothy 2:4). God did not just *proclaim* His desire that none should perish. He *proved* His desire to save people when He left the glories of heaven, in the person of Jesus and came to earth to die on the cross for our sins (John 3:16, Romans 5:8). Having paid the penalty for mankind's rebellion, God now graciously offers forgiveness and everlasting life as a free gift (Romans 6:23) to all who will put their trust in Jesus.

If someone rejects God's grace, turns away from the testimony of their own conscience (Romans 2:15), the testimony of creation (Psalm 19:1-6, Acts 14:16-17), the wooing of the Holy Spirit (John 16:8) and says, "I will have nothing to do with God," God will, in the end, allow them to have their wish (2 Thessalonians 1:9). As C. S. Lewis said, "The damned are, in one sense, successful, rebels to the end...the doors of hell are locked on the *inside*."[23] In the end, those people who end up in hell will have only themselves to blame. Hell is the end of a path that is chosen, to some degree, in this life right here and now, day by day.[24]

THY WILL BE DONE:

"There are only two kinds of people in the end: those who say to God, 'Thy will be done,' and those to whom God says, in the end, '*Thy* will be done.'"

–**C. S. Lewis** (1898-1963), Professor of Medieval and Renaissance Literature at the University of Cambridge; *The Great Divorce*, 1946, p. 72.

11 "Haven't certain books of the Bible been lost?"

No. The supposedly "lost books" of the Bible that have been found, the so-called gospels of Thomas, Philip, and Mary Magdalene, were not *lost* gospels, they were *pseudo* gospels that the early church rejected as uninspired, spurious writings. The Christian church was familiar with these documents, but purposely left them out of the Bible, easily recognizing that they were not divinely inspired.

We too can be certain these books do not belong in the Bible. Why? *First*, they were not written by any of the apostles or their close associates (e.g., Mark or Luke). Most scholars, Christian and non-Christian, date these Gnostic gospels to the second and third centuries, *long after* the time of Christ. *Secondly,* these writings contradict authentic revelation.[25]

You can be absolutely confident that God, who inspired (2 Timothy 3:16) the men to pen the words of the Bible (2 Peter 1:21), saw to it that none of the inspired writings were lost. It would be foolish for us to think that an all-knowing, all-powerful God could lose track of books He intended to put in the Bible, or anything else for that matter.

ON THE BIBLE:

"I must say, that having for many years made the evidences of Christianity the subject of close study, the result has been a firm and increasing conviction of the authenticity and plenary inspiration of the Bible. It is indeed the Word of God."

–Simon Greenleaf (1783-1853), Professor and Founder of Harvard Law School; in correspondence with the American Bible Society, November 6, 1852.

"For eighteen centuries every engine of destruction that human science, philosophy, wit, reasoning or brutality could bring to bear against a book has been brought to bear against that book to stamp it out of the world, but it has a mightier hold on the world today than ever before. If that were man's book it would have been annihilated and forgotten hundreds of years ago..."

–R. A. Torrey (1856-1928), Dean of the Bible Institute of Los Angeles, author of more than forty books; "Ten Reasons Why I Believe the Bible is the Word of God," 1898, Reason 5.

12

"Isn't there a conflict between the God in the Old Testament, who is often portrayed as cruel, and the God of the New Testament who seems very loving?"

Not at all. The God of the Old Testament is the very same loving God spoken of in the New Testament. The Old Testament says He is, "gracious and merciful; slow to anger and great in lovingkindness" (Psalm 145:8, NASB) and God says in Malachi 3:6, "I am the LORD, I do not change."

The Old Testament does, perhaps, contain more stories of God's judgment against sinners than the New Testament (e.g., the Flood, the destruction of Sodom and Gomorrah). Keep in mind though that the Old Testament covers about four thousand years of history and the New Testament covers less than a hundred years.

The God spoken of in the New Testament is just as serious about sin as He was in the Old Testament. The New Testament tells of a time when God's judgment is going to come upon the whole earth in the last days (Matthew 24:21, 2 Peter 3:7, Revelation 6-18). Beyond that, the New Testament clearly talks about a time when unrepentant, unforgiven sinners will stand before God to be judged for their sins (Revelation 20:12-15).

ON THE BIBLE:

"I have a fundamental belief in the Bible as the Word of God, written by those who were inspired. I study the Bible daily."

–Sir Isaac Newton (1642-1727), English physicist, mathematician, astronomer, inventor, philosopher and alchemist, widely regarded as one of the most influential scientists in history. Quote cited at http://www.answers.com/topic/sir-isaac-newton.

ON EVOLUTION:

"In grammar school they taught me that a frog turning into a prince was a fairy tale. In the university they taught me that a frog turning into a prince was a fact."

–Ron Carlson, Christian apologist. Quote cited in *I Don't Have Enough Faith To Be An Atheist* by Dr. Norman Geisler and Frank Turek, 2004, p. 137.

13

"Why do Christians reject the apocryphal writings[26] that are in the Catholic Bible?"

There are numerous reasons why Christians (including those making up the early church) have rejected the apocryphal books as authoritative or divinely inspired. Let me share with you four reasons.[27]

First, the apocryphal writings contain numerous teachings that contradict authentic Scripture (e.g., praying for the dead, the doctrine of purgatory, the teaching that salvation is available through good works and the giving of alms). *Secondly*, the apocryphal writings contain numerous historical, geographical and chronological errors.[28] *Thirdly*, Jesus and the apostles cite the Old Testament nearly three hundred times in the pages of the New Testament (referring to it as Scripture); they never quote any of the apocryphal books accepted by the Roman Catholic Church.[29] *Fourthly*, the apocryphal writings were never included in the Hebrew Bible. The Jews themselves, from whom the apocryphal writings came, did not accept the writings as divinely inspired. The apocryphal writings were not formally declared to be authoritative and inspired by the Catholic Church until the Council of Trent in A.D. 1546. The Catholic Church's acceptance of these writings into the canon of Scripture was an effort to counter the teachings of Martin Luther and the other leaders of the Reformation. These men were pointing out that many teachings of the Catholic Church came from the Apocrypha, not the sixty-six books of the Bible.

ON THE AUTHORITY OF THE SCRIPTURES:

"Unless I am convinced by Scripture and plain reason–I do not accept the authority of the popes and councils, for they have contradicted each other–my conscience is captive to the Word of God. I cannot and I will not recant anything for to go against conscience is neither right nor safe. Here I stand. I can do no other. God help me. Amen."

–**Martin Luther** (1483-1546), German priest and scholar whose questioning of certain Roman Catholic church practices led to the Protestant Reformation. Words above were spoken at his trial at the Diet of Worms, April 18, 1521.

14 "Doesn't the Bible have a bunch of contradictions in it?"

No. There *are* some verses in the Bible that seem to contradict one another, but with a little investigation into the original languages, the context of the various passages and the cultural and geographical settings in which the Bible was originally written, they are cleared up. Here is an example. Luke 18:35 says that Jesus healed a blind man as He "was coming *near* Jericho." Mark 10:46 says Jesus healed the man "as He went *out* of Jericho." So, the critics have said, "Surely Luke or Mark made a mistake." That does appear to be the case. What is the solution?

A German archaeologist by the name of Ernest

Sellin, working on an excavation in Israel between 1907 and 1909, discovered that there were actually what have been called "the twin-cities" of Jericho in Jesus' time. There was the old city of Jericho (from the Old Testament story of Joshua) and the new Roman city of Jericho. The two cities, both called Jericho, were separated from one another by about a mile. Knowing that there were two cities called Jericho in Jesus' day solves the apparent contradiction. Luke referred to the city that Jesus was *approaching*. Mark referred to the one that Jesus had *left*. The healing of the blind man occurred as Jesus traveled between the two. It is not the gospel writers who erred, but the critics of the Bible who are unfamiliar with first century Roman and Jewish geography.[30]

ON THE GOSPELS:

"All I am in private life is a literary critic and historian, that's my job....And I'm prepared to say on that basis if anyone thinks the Gospels are either legends or novels, then that person is simply showing his incompetence as a literary critic. I've read a great many novels and I know a fair amount about the legends that grew up among early people, and I know perfectly well the Gospels are not that kind of stuff."

–**C. S. Lewis** (1898-1963), Professor of Medieval and Renaissance Literature at the University of Cambridge; *Christian Reflections*, 1967, p. 209.

15

"Wasn't the New Testament written down hundreds of years *after* Jesus lived? Wouldn't that make it unreliable?"

There is actually good evidence that most of the New Testament was completed before A.D. 70.[31] For example, the New Testament Scriptures are absolutely silent regarding the destruction of the Jewish temple by the Romans in A.D. 70. This was one of the most significant events in all of Jewish history, and even something that Jesus prophesied would happen (Mark 13:1-2). The silence of the New Testament authors implies that their writings were completed prior to this event.

Secondly, the New Testament authors, who

on numerous occasions mentioned the names of rulers like Herod, Caiaphas, and Pontius Pilate, are completely silent regarding Caesar Nero and the incredible persecution he unleashed on the church in A.D. 64.

Thirdly, the martyrdoms of Paul (A.D. 64) and Peter (A.D. 65) are not mentioned anywhere in the New Testament. The apostle Paul was still alive at the end of Luke's *second* writing, the book of Acts (see Acts 28). This implies that Luke's first writing, his Gospel, must have been done sometime prior.

Fourthly, John mentions the pool of Bethesda (John 5:2), which was destroyed in A.D. 70, as still being in existence at the time he wrote his Gospel. I could go on,[32] but it is safe to say that the New Testament was completed before the close of the first century, within the lifetimes of the eyewitnesses and contemporaries of the events.

ON THE BIBLE:

"Holy Scripture could never lie or err...its decrees are of absolute and inavoidable truth."

–Galileo Galilei (1564-1642), Italian physicist, astronomer, and philosopher who is referred to as the "father of modern astronomy," the "father of modern physics," and the "father of science;" in a letter to Benedetto Castelli, of the University of Pisa, in 1613.

"Men do not reject the Bible because it contradicts itself, but because it contradicts them."

–E. Paul Hovey

16

"Doesn't the Bible have scientific errors in it?"

The Bible may appear slightly out of harmony with some modern day *theories*, like the theory of Darwinian evolution, but when it comes to actual verifiable, provable scientific *facts*, there is perfect harmony between the Bible and the way things really are. Not only did the authors of the Bible speak accurately about the universe in which we live, they made known numerous facts about the universe thousands of years before modern scientists actually discovered them. I will give you three quick examples.

The first example has to do with the earth's *shape*.

About 2,600 years ago, when most of the world thought the earth was flat, Isaiah declared that the earth was actually a round sphere (Isaiah 40:22).

A second example has to do with the earth's *suspension*. Job, the author of one of the oldest books in the Bible, proclaimed more than 4,000 years ago that the earth hangs "on *nothing*" (Job 26:7). It was not until 1650 that scientists discovered that to be true. Hindus believed that the earth rested on the back of an elephant, which stood on the back of a turtle that was swimming in a great endless sea. The Greeks believed that the mythical god Atlas carried the earth on his shoulders!

A third example has to do with the *sun*. The Qur'an, written in the seventh century A.D., says that the sun sets in a muddy spring (Surah 18:86) but David, writing about 1,700 years before Muhammad, said that the sun is actually on a circuit "from one end of heaven...to the other end" (Psalm 19:6).

How did Isaiah, Job and David know these things? 2 Peter 1:21 tells us that, "holy men of God spoke as they were moved by the Holy Spirit." God, who knows all there is to know about the universe and the earth that He created, supernaturally superintended the authors of the Bible to make sure that what He wanted written was actually written.

17

"How do you know that Christianity is true and not some other religion like Buddhism or Islam?"

Jesus said it was. Jesus testified that the Bible, upon which Christianity is based, was without error (John 17:17), historically reliable (cf. Matthew 12:40, 24:37-39), divinely authoritative (Matthew 4:4-10), scientifically accurate regarding the origin of man (Matthew19:4-5), infallible (John 10:35) and indestructible (Matthew 5:18). If Jesus was a prophet of God, as even the Qur'an teaches,[33] or even if He was a good teacher,[34] as so many are willing to believe, it would be wise for us to take His word on the matter. Jesus *proved* that He was the trustworthy Son of God by: His miraculous fulfillment of hundreds of Old Testament prophecies,[35] His sinless life,[36] His miracles[37] and His resurrection from the dead.[38] Buddha and Muhammad both admitted their sinfulness,[39] performed no miracles, and both of their bodies are in their tombs to this day. Jesus' grave is empty.[40] He is the reliable authority on life after death and spiritual matters.

ON THE RESURRECTION:

"I have been used for many years to study the histories of other times, and to examine and weigh the evidence of those who have written about them, and I know of no one fact in the history of mankind which is proved by better and fuller evidence of every sort, to the understanding of a fair inquirer, than the great sign which God hath given us that Christ died and rose again from the dead."

–**Thomas Arnold** (1795-1842), Regius Professor of Modern History at Oxford University and author of the famous three volume *History of Rome*. Quote cited in *Evidence That Demands A Verdict* (Vol. 1) by Josh McDowell, 1979, p. 191.

"The evidence for the resurrection is better than for claimed miracles in any other religion. It's outstandingly different in quality and quantity."

–**Antony Flew, Ph.D.** (1923-), British philosopher, author, debater and former atheist; interview with Gary Habermas, 2004. See www.biola.edu/antonyflew.

18

"What about homosexuals? Do you believe that they go to hell?"

The Bible says that *anybody* who refuses to turn from their sin and receive God's forgiveness will end up in hell, whether they be a heterosexual or homosexual. Does the Bible teach that homosexuality is a sin? Yes, very clearly (see Leviticus 18:22, 1 Corinthians 6:9-10, Romans 1:26-28), but it also says that fornication (sex between an unmarried man and woman), lying, stealing, and drunkenness are sins. So, let us lay aside the whole issue of homosexuality for a moment and imagine that our homosexual friends are married, monogamous heterosexuals. They still have a problem. They, like all of us (Psalm 143:2), have broken a number of God's other commandments. No matter the sin, every person, heterosexual or homosexual, must turn to the Lord and trust in Christ, in order to be saved (Acts 4:12, 17:30-31).[41]

ON SPEAKING WITH SKEPTICS:

"I confess that when I have to argue about the truth of divine things it is a dreary task to me....while they are wanting me to argue about this point or that it seems to me like asking a man to prove that there is a sun in yonder sky. I bask in His beams, I swoon under His heat, I see by His light; and yet they ask me to prove His existence! Are the men mad? What do they want me to prove? That God hears prayer? I pray and receive answers every day. That God pardons sin? I was in my own esteem the blackest of sinners, and sunk in the depths of despair, yet I believed, and by that faith I leaped into a fulness of light and liberty at once. Why do they not try it themselves?"

–Charles H. Spurgeon (1834-1892), British preacher.

19

"How do you know that Jesus rose from the dead?"

Here are a few quick reasons. *First*, there was the amazing rise of Christianity 2,000 years ago, right in the very city where the people demanded Jesus' crucifixion, and where Jesus was publicly crucified and buried. The best explanation for the sudden birth of Christianity and its phenomenal growth is that Jesus really did rise from the dead.

Secondly, there were the agonizing deaths that the early Christians were willing to suffer, in order to testify that Jesus was alive.[42] The best explanation for their boldness and willingness to die was that they really did see Jesus alive after His crucifixion

(1 Corinthians 15:3-7). Nobody willingly and knowingly dies for a lie.

Thirdly, the Old Testament prophesied that the Messiah *would* rise from the dead (Psalm 16:10) and the New Testament says that Jesus *did* rise from the dead (Matthew 28:6). Hundreds of fulfilled prophecies, thousands of archaeological discoveries and dozens of external sources (e.g., Flavius Josephus) have established the fact that the Bible is, at bare minimum, a historically reliable book.

Fourthly, I would tell you about my own personal experience. Years ago I cried out to Jesus and said, "If You are alive, come into my life, forgive me of my sins, and be the Lord of my life." Many things since then have convinced me, beyond the shadow of a doubt, that He heard that prayer and is indeed alive and at work in my life.[43]

ON THE RESURRECTION:

"Why would the apostles lie?....Liars always lie for selfish reasons. If they lied, what was their motive, what did they get out of it? What they got out of it was misunderstanding, rejection, persecution, torture, and martyrdom. Hardly a list of perks!"

–**Peter Kreeft, Ph.D.,** Professor of Philosophy at Boston College. *Why I Am A Christian: Leading Thinkers Explain Why They Believe* edited by Norman L. Geisler and Paul K. Hoffman, 2001, p. 232.

20 "What about evolution? Haven't Darwin's theories disproved God's existence?"

Let's suppose that Darwin's theory of evolution was true. Would that disprove God's existence? Not at all, for one might reason (although I would disagree) that it was *God* who used the process of evolution to bring about the current world we live in. If you hold to Darwin's theories, do not allow that to keep you back from acknowledging that you are a sinner and in need of God's grace and forgiveness.

Darwin's theory is a theory in crisis. More and more scientists from universities such as Princeton, U.C. Berkeley, Cambridge, M.I.T., and so on, are acknowledging that life is far too complex to have come about by random mutation and natural selection.[44] Scientists are beginning to acknowledge that not even a single living cell could have come into being apart from an intelligent maker,[45] it is that complex. Even the well-known atheist, Carl Sagan, marveled at the complexity of the human cell saying, "A living cell is a marvel of detailed and complex architecture....The information content of a simple cell had been estimated as around 10^{12} bits, comparable to about a hundred million pages of the Encyclopedia Britannica."[46]

There is a book that I recommend you read. It is called *Icons of Evolution—Science or Myth?*[47] by Dr. Jonathan Wells, a scientist who earned his Ph.D. in Molecular and Cell Biology from U.C. Berkeley and a second Ph.D. from Yale University. In this book he demonstrates how the evidence scientists have held up for evolution has been exaggerated and even fabricated. This book is shaking the Darwinian establishment at its foundation.

ON EVOLUTION:

"To suppose that the eye, with all its inimitable contrivances for adjusting the focus to different distances, for admitting different amounts of light, and for the correction of spherical and chromatic aberration, could have been formed by natural selection, seems, I freely confess, absurd in the highest possible degree."

–**Charles Darwin** (1809-1882), British naturalist; *The Origin of Species*, 1859, chapter 6, online edition at http://www.literature.org.

21

"If everything needs a maker, as Christians seem to suggest, then who made God?"

Nobody. Everything that *begins* to exist does require a cause, but the Bible says that God is Spirit (John 4:24) and eternal, or without beginning (Psalm 90:2). That being the case, He did not need a maker, or a cause. He is the Uncaused Cause, or Creator, of all things (Isaiah 44:24, John 1:3).

ON EVIDENCE FOR A DESIGNER:

"It now seems to me that the findings of more than fifty years of DNA research have provided materials for a new and enormously powerful argument to design."

—**Antony Flew, Ph.D.** (1923-), British philosopher, author, debater and former atheist; interview with Gary Habermas, 2004. See www.biola.edu/antonyflew.

"There is for me powerful evidence that there is something going on behind it all....It seems as though somebody has fine tuned nature's numbers to make the Universe....The impression of design is overwhelming."

—**Paul Davies, Ph.D.** (1946-), internationally acclaimed physicist and author, who has held previous academic appointments at the Universities of Cambridge, London, and Adelaide; *The Cosmic Blueprint*, 1988, p. 203.

ON EVOLUTION:

"Scientists who utterly reject evolution may be one of our fastest-growing controversial minorities... Many of the scientists supporting this position hold impressive credentials in science."

—**Larry Hatfield,** "Educators Against Darwin," *Science Digest* (Winter 1979), pp. 94-96.

22

"Well, if God doesn't need a maker [see previous question and answer], why couldn't we just say that the universe doesn't need a maker either?"

God does not need a maker because He has always been. The universe has not always been. An overwhelming amount of evidence including the motion of the galaxies, the Second Law of Thermodynamics, and the background radiation echo, proves that it began to exist a finite time ago. This fact is hardly debated within the scientific community. Logically, we know that anything that begins to exist must have a cause or a maker. Even David Hume, one of the most zealous skeptics of

Christianity ever, agreed to this fact when he said, "I never asserted so absurd a proposition as that anything might arise without a cause."[48] If the universe began to exist, and we know that it did, it must have a cause or maker. Nothing cannot, and does not, produce something.[49]

ON THE UNIVERSE:

"I myself find it hard to accept the notion of self-creation *from nothing*, even given unrestricted chance."

−J. L. Mackie (1917-1981), atheistic philosopher, author, a fellow of University College, Oxford; *Times Literary Supplement*, 1982, p. 126.

ON DIFFICULTIES IN BELIEVING:

"I have noticed that whenever a person gives up his belief in the Word of God because it requires that he should believe a good deal, his unbelief requires him to believe a great deal more. If there be any difficulties in the faith of Christ, they are not one-tenth as great as the absurdities in any system of unbelief which seeks to take its place."

−Charles H. Spurgeon (1834-1892), British preacher.

23 "Can God make a rock so big that He cannot move it? Yes or No?"

With the way you have worded the question a simple "Yes" or "No" answer will not work. Either answer would suggest that God is not omnipotent (all-powerful), something the Bible clearly affirms (Genesis 18:14, Luke 1:37). Your question is like asking someone, "Have you stopped beating your wife yet? Yes or No?" For the person who has not been beating his wife, a simple yes or no answer will not do. If he says yes, he implies that he used to beat his wife. If he says no, he lies and implies that he is still beating his wife. The same is true with this question. A yes or no answer will not work. I will answer your question this way; God, because He is omnipotent, can create any kind of rock that He wants to and because He is omnipotent, He can lift any rock that He creates.[50]

ON APPARENT DESIGN:

"A common sense interpretation of the facts suggests that a superintellect has monkeyed with physics, as well as with chemistry and biology, and that there are no blind forces worth speaking about in nature. The numbers one calculates from the facts seem to me so overwhelming as to put this conclusion almost beyond question."

–Fred Hoyle, Ph.D. (1915-2001), world-renowned British astronomer and Professor of Astronomy at Cambridge University; *The Universe: Some Past and Present Reflections*, 1982, 20:16.

ON THE FOSSIL RECORD:

"The extreme rarity of transitional forms in the fossil record persists as the trade secret of paleontology. The evolutionary trees that adorn our textbooks have data only at the tips and nodes of their branches; the rest is inference, however reasonable, *not the evidence of fossils*."

–Stephen Jay Gould, Ph.D. (1941-2002), evolutionist, author, paleontologist, Professor at Harvard University; *The Panda's Thumb*, 1982, p. 181. Emphasis added.

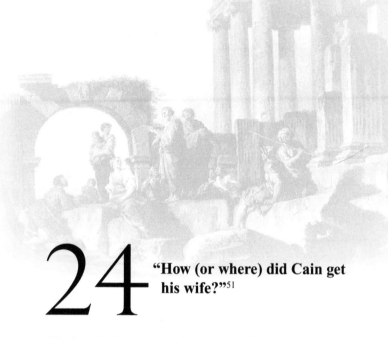

24

"How (or where) did Cain get his wife?"[51]

Obviously, he married someone in Adam and Eve's lineage, perhaps a sister, or a niece. The three boys mentioned in Genesis 4, Cain, Abel and Seth, were not the only children Adam and Eve had. The very next chapter says that Adam and Eve had, "other sons and daughters" (Genesis 5:4, NASB). Some critics say, "Aha, but didn't God forbid incest?" No, not at that time. It was only later, during the days of Moses (c. 1446 B.C.[52]), after the gene pool had undergone years of contamination by sin, that the Lord forbade incest (see Leviticus 18-20).[53]

ON ERRORS IN INTERPRETING THE BIBLE

"...in my experience when critics raise these objections, they invariably violate one of seventeen principles for interpreting the Scriptures....For example, assuming the unexplained is unexplainable....failing to understand the context of the passage....assuming a partial report is a false report...neglecting to interpret difficult passages in light of clear ones; basing a teaching on an obscure passage; forgetting that the Bible uses nontechnical, everyday language; failing to remember the Bible uses different literary devices..."

–Norman Geisler, Ph.D., author or coauthor of more than sixty books, including *When Critics Ask,* a popular handbook addressing alleged errors and apparent contradicitons in the Bible. Quote above taken from his interview in *The Case for Faith* by Lee Strobel, 2000, pp. 137-138.

ON ARCHAEOLOGY:

"It may be stated categorically that no archaeological discovery has ever controverted a Biblical reference. Scores of archeological findings have been made which confirm in clear outline or exact detail historical statements in the Bible. And, by the same token, proper evaluation of Biblical descriptions has often led to amazing discoveries."

–Nelson Glueck, Ph.D. (1900–1971), renowned archaeologist, author, discoverer of more than 1,000 sites in the Middle East, appeared on the cover of TIME Magazine in 1963; *Rivers in the Desert*, 1959, p. 136.

25 "How can you adhere to a religion that would advocate such events as the Crusades?"

The Crusades, of nearly a thousand years ago, were certainly carried out in the name of Christianity, but the violence that occurred was carried out in direct disobedience to the teachings of Christ. Jesus told His disciples to love their enemies (Matthew 5:44). As Jesus was being arrested on the eve of His crucifixion, Peter pulled out his sword and struck the ear of Malchus, the servant of the high priest. Jesus healed the man's ear and told Peter to put away his sword (John 18:11). Even as Jesus was dying on the cross, He asked His Father to forgive His murderers (Luke 23:34). God's kingdom was not, nor is it now, to be advanced with violence. Do not let the unchristian behavior of men a thousand years ago, keep you from receiving God's free gift (Romans 6:23) of eternal life!

ON JESUS:

"Alexander, Caesar, Charlemagne, and myself founded empires; but upon what foundation did we rest the creations of our genius? Upon force! But Jesus Christ founded His upon love; and at this hour millions of men would die for Him."
–**Napoleon Bonaparte I** (1769-1821), Emperor of France from 1804 to 1815. *America's God and Country: Encyclopedia of Quotations*, 1994, p. 463.

ON THE BIBLE:

"We are fortunate to have the Bible and especially the New Testament, which tells us so much about God in widely accessible human terms."
–**Arthur Schawlow, Ph.D.** (1921-1999), professor of physics at Stanford University, Physics Nobel Prize winner (1981), honored for his work in laser spectroscopy. Quote cited in "Stephen Hawking, the Big Bang, and God," by Henry F. Schaefer, III.

26

"What about the Old Testament, when Joshua and the nation of Israel were commanded by God to go through the land of Canaan and destroy everyone? How can you believe in a God who would command such a thing?"

There are at least three things that we need to remember when we consider the story of Joshua. *First*, God is sovereign over His creation. He created us and He has the right to do with us as He deems best. If you plant a garden in your backyard, you have the right to do with it as you see fit. You can pluck those plants up whenever you want. Your neighbor does not have that right. Why? Those plants do not belong to him. The same is true with God. People belong to God and He can end a life, or lives, whenever and however He thinks best.

Secondly, the people of Canaan were guilty of terrible sins. They were burning their children as sacrifices to the god Molech. They were having sexual relations with animals (Leviticus 18:21-24). They hated the Hebrew people and would have destroyed them. This would have prohibited the Messiah, the future Savior for all mankind, from being born into the world, for it was promised that He would be a descendant of Abraham.

Thirdly, keep in mind that God patiently allowed the people of Canaan over four hundred years to repent (Genesis 15:16-21). Had they repented, like the people of Nineveh did (Jonah 3), God would have spared them (Jeremiah 18:7-8).

ON THE BIBLE:

"There are more sure marks of authenticity in the Bible than in any profane history."
—**Sir Isaac Newton** (1642-1727), English physicist, mathematician, astronomer, inventor, philosopher and alchemist, widely regarded as one of the most influential scientists in history. *America's God and Country: Encyclopedia of Quotations*, 1994, p. 473.

27 "Do you think that it's right to try and force your beliefs upon other people?"

No. Nowhere in the Gospels do we see Jesus coercing people to believe. The New Testament tells us that, "He went through every city and village, preaching and bringing the glad tidings of the kingdom of God" (Luke 8:1). He simply shared the good news, and that is what He sent out His disciples to do (Luke 9:2). Jesus does not kick doors down and force Himself into a person's life (Revelation 3:20). He waits to be received (John 1:12). He allows people to freely (John 5:39-40, Matthew 22:3) choose whom they will follow (Joshua 24:15, Matthew 23:37).

So, is it right to try and force our beliefs upon

a person? No. Is it right to humbly, gently, respect-fully[54] share the good news about all that God has done? Absolutely. After that, it is up to the individual to decide whether or not to believe.

ON TRUTH:

"Truth is so obscured nowadays and lies [are] so well established that unless we love the truth we shall never recognize it."

—Blaise Pascal (1623-1662), mathematician, French scientist, Christian, philosopher; *Pensées*, in *Christianity for Modern Pagans: Pascal's Pensées*, by Peter Kreeft, 1993, p. 216.

"If you abide in My word, you are My disciples indeed. And you shall know the truth, and the truth shall make you free."

—Jesus Christ; The Gospel of John, 8:31-32

ON ATHEIST'S CONVERSION:

"I heard the story of a man, a blasphemer...an atheist, who was converted singularly by a sinful action of his. He had written on a piece of paper, "God is nowhere," and ordered his child to read it, for he would make him an atheist too. The child spelled it, "God is n-o-w h-e-r-e. God is now here." It was a truth instead of a lie, and the arrow pierced the man's own heart."

—Charles H. Spurgeon (1834-1892), British preacher.

28 "Where did the dinosaurs come from? Didn't dinosaurs live millions of years before man?"

The Bible teaches that God made everything that has ever existed in the universe (Exodus 20:11, Genesis 1, John 1:3). This would include the stars, planets, animals, fish, people, and all that there is, including dinosaurs.

To answer the second part of your question, Didn't dinosaurs live millions of years before man? The answer is no. The Bible teaches (Genesis 1:24-31) that God made all the land dwelling creatures, which would have included dinosaurs and the first humans, Adam and Eve, on the sixth day of creation. So, based on the inspired, infallible Word of God, we believe that man and dinosaurs coexisted at the same time. The Old Testament authors spoke of creatures that were huge, having tails like cedar trees (Job 40:17), probably referring to one of the larger dinosaurs that used to roam the earth (see answer to question 29).

There appears to be extrabiblical evidence surfacing that man and dinosaurs *did* coexist. One example would be the ancient Indian rock drawings (petroglyphs) that have been found at the Natural Bridges National Monument in Utah, depicting men interacting with dinosaurs.[55]

ON ATHEIST'S CHANGE OF MIND:

"When I began my career as a cosmologist some twenty years ago, I was a convinced atheist. I never in my wildest dreams imagined that one day I would be writing a book purporting to show that the central claims of Judeo-Christian theology are in fact true, that these claims are straightforward deductions of the laws of physics as we now understand them. I have been forced into these conclusions by the inexorable logic of my own special branch of physics."

–**Frank J. Tipler, Ph.D.**, author, Professor of Mathematical Physics at Tulane University, Oxford University Senior Research Fellow (1979); *The Physics Of Immortality*, 1994, Preface.

29 "Why aren't dinosaurs mentioned in the Bible?"

First, we should not expect to see the word *dinosaur* in the Bible. The term was not coined until a famous paleontologist, Sir Richard Owen, gave them that name in 1841–nearly eighteen centuries after the New Testament was finished.[56]

Second, just because a creature is not mentioned in the Bible does not mean that it did not exist. There are thousands of creatures that are not specifically mentioned in the Bible: giraffes, alligators, penguins, just to name a few.

Thirdly, the Bible does actually mention at least two different creatures that very well may have been dinosaurs: Behemoth, and Leviathan. Behemoth is described as having a tail like a cedar tree (Job 40:15-19). Of Leviathan, the Lord said to Job, "... indeed, any hope of overcoming him is false; Shall one not be overwhelmed at the sight of him? No one is so fierce that he would dare stir him up....Who can remove his outer coat? Who can approach him with a double bridle? Who can open the doors of his face, with his terrible teeth all around? His rows of scales are his pride" (Job 41:9-10, 13-15a). Scales? Terrible teeth? So fierce that no one would dare wake him up? It is easy to see why numerous Biblical scholars have concluded that Leviathan may have been a dinosaur.

ON INTELLIGENT DESIGN

"When you analyze all of the most current affirmative evidence from cosmology, physics, astronomy, biology, and so forth...the positive case for an intelligent designer becomes absolutely compelling."

–Jonathan Wells, Ph.D., scientist, earned a Ph.D. in molecular and cell biology from U.C. Berkeley and another Ph.D. from Yale University. Interview with Lee Strobel, *The Case for a Creator*, 2004, p. 66.

"The most beautiful system of the sun, planets and comets could only proceed from the counsel and dominion of an intelligent and powerful being."

–Sir Isaac Newton (1642-1727), English physicist, mathematician, astronomer, inventor, philosopher and alchemist, widely regarded as one of the most influential scientists in history; *Principia, Book III*; cited in *Newton's Philosophy of Nature: Selections from his writings*, 1953, p. 42.

30

"How could dinosaurs fit on Noah's ark? If dinosaurs *were* on Noah's ark, why aren't they around today?"

Those are great questions. *First*, bear in mind that the ark described in the Bible was not the 45' – 50' model made popular in children's books. It was extremely large. According to the measurements given in the Bible (Genesis 6:15) it was about 450 feet long, 75 feet wide and 45 feet tall (4.5 stories)!

Secondly, remember that not all dinosaurs were large like the Brachiosaurus. Many of them, like the Compsognathus, were quite small, even just a few pounds. Even the biggest dinosaurs came from eggs no larger than footballs.[57]

Thirdly, it is likely that Noah took young dinosaurs with him, rather than the older and larger ones. The smaller ones would have been easier to fit in the ark, to feed, to take care of, and would have been in better shape than older ones for repopulating the earth.

Fourthly, remember that Noah was not required to bring two of every *type* of dinosaur on the ark, but only two of every *kind* (Genesis 6:20), a much smaller number.[58] Fitting the dinosaurs on the ark would have been no problem.[59]

As for why we do not see dinosaurs around today, keep in mind that the Flood occurred approximately 2,300-2,400 years before Christ, more than 4,000 years ago. As for those dinosaurs that survived the Flood aboard Noah's ark, we are not sure why their offspring did not continue indefinitely. They may have died off for some of the same reasons other creatures have become extinct. Perhaps they were over hunted. Perhaps an ice age or severe change in the environment that came after the Flood affected the lush vegetation that many of them depended upon for food. Only God knows for sure. The existence of billions of dead animals, including dinosaurs, encased in sedimentary rock (which interestingly, is rock that has been laid down by water) averaging a mile deep[60] on all seven continents, is an amazing evidence that the Flood (Genesis 6:17, 7:4) actually did occur.

31 "How could all the races, with their different skin colors, come from Noah's family?"

There are two facts that we need to keep in mind when we consider this question.[61] *First*, there is only one race, the human race. The Chinese, Africans, Eskimos, Indians, and Australian Aborigines are all homo sapiens. When it comes to the basic structure of the human body, all of these groups have the same amount of bones, the same organs, and can all successfully interbreed with one another. The primary difference between these different groups is their skin color.

Secondly, keep in mind, there is really only one skin color: melanin. Melanin is the brownish pigment that we all have in our skin that protects the skin from the sun's damaging ultraviolet light. If a person's body only produces a little melanin, he will have fairer skin. If their body produces a lot of melanin, they will be dark brown. In between are all the lighter shades of brown. God created our bodies with an amazing ability to adapt to our environment. People groups who have long lived in colder climates (e.g., northern Europe), where there is not much sunlight, have developed fairer skin. People groups who have lived nearer to the equator (e.g., Africa), where the sun is more intense, have developed darker skin.

Why would God design humans with this built in capability? It is important for our survival. If you have too little melanin in your skin (you are fair skinned) and live in a very sunny environment, you will easily burn and develop skin cancer. If you have a great deal of melanin (darker skin), and you live in a country where there is little sunshine (Finland for example), it will be harder for you to get enough vitamin D, which needs sunshine for its production in your body. Having a vitamin D deficiency can cause bone disorders such as rickets.

32 "Don't all religions basically teach the same thing?"

That is a popular belief, but the answer is no. The religions of the world are vastly different, and even contradictory, in many of their core teachings.

For example, consider some of the different views when it comes to the *nature* of God. Some religions, like Islam, Christianity and Judaism, teach that God is the transcendent creator of the world, and as such, He is distinct and separate from his creation. Some religions, like Hinduism, teach that God and the physical universe are one and the same. Some religions teach that God is a *he*, some say a *she*, some say an *it*. Mormonism, Shinto, and different tribal religions teach that there are many gods. Adherents to the New Age Movement and Christian Science believe that *we* are God.

Consider the different views of *salvation* and what that even means. Judaism, Islam and Christianity teach that salvation means eternal life in heaven. To Buddhists it means an indescribable, almost nonexistent state known as parinirvana. To the majority of Jehovah's Witnesses it means everlasting life on earth. The goal of Hindus is to break free from the cycle of life, death and reincarnation and have their individual personality annihilated by becoming absorbed into Brahman.

Consider *how salvation* is obtained. The Bible teaches that salvation is a free gift given by a gracious God to all who receive it by faith. The Qur'an says salvation can be obtained if you submit yourself to Allah and His laws and your good works outweigh your bad works. Hinduism's ultimate goal is to be obtained by achieving a certain state of consciousness in which one realizes his or her identity with God. Buddhism's ultimate goal is said to be achievable to those who eliminate all desires, even the desire to live.

When it comes to the nature of God, salvation, and how that salvation is obtained, the world's religions contain many contradictory teachings.

33

"Don't Christians worship the same God as Muslims?"

No. There are some major differences between the god presented in the Qur'an and the God of the Bible. The Qur'an teaches that Allah is not triune in nature (Father, Son and Holy Spirit) like the God of the Bible. To say that God has a Son, as the Bible does, is an unforgivable sin known as *shirk* to Muslims.[62]

Another thing that sets the true and living God apart from the god put forth in the Qur'an is His love. The Qur'an states over and over again that Allah does not love ungrateful sinners, unbelievers, the proud, or the extravagant.[63] The God of the Bible loves the whole world, including sinners. Jesus said, "For God so loved the *world* [that would include everyone] that He gave His only begotten Son, that whoever believes in Him should not perish but have everlasting life" (John 3:16). The Bible says elsewhere that, "God demonstrates His own love toward us, in that while we were yet *sinners*, Christ died for us" (Romans 5:8, NASB). That is good news for those of us who realize we are sinners.

The Bible also teaches that those who put their faith in Christ are adopted into God's family (Ephesians 1:5) and can personally address God as "Father," (Matthew 6:9, Romans 8:15). The God of the Bible offers mankind a personal relationship of great intimacy. That is not the case in Islam. In Islam there is no fatherly concept of God. To most Muslims, Allah is seen more as a remote judge, who is not personally involved with mankind. Islam is not about fellowship *with* God, but service, submission and allegiance *to* God.[64]

These are just some of the differences between the god put forth in the Qur'an and the God of the Bible. The god portrayed in the Qur'an is not the God spoken of in the Bible, and in fact, does not even exist (Isaiah 46:9).

ON GOD:

"I, even I, am the LORD, and besides Me there is no savior....I am God, and there is no other; I am God, and there is none like Me."

—God, Isaiah 43:11, 46:9

34

"What makes you think that the Qur'an is not divinely inspired?"

There are numerous reasons.[65] *First*, it contradicts authentic Scripture, the Bible. For instance, it teaches that God does not love sinners (e.g., Surah 2:276), and that salvation is obtained by a person's good works outweighing bad works (Surah 23:102-3). The Bible teaches that God loves sinners (Romans 5:8) and that salvation comes to us solely through God's grace (Ephesians 2:8-9).

Secondly, it contradicts known facts of science. For example, it teaches that the sun actually descends down into the earth, into a muddy spring (Surah 18:86). You could get away with a statement like that in certain parts of the world in the seventh century. Obviously, today, we know that the sun is actually on a circuit through space.[66]

Thirdly, the Qur'an contradicts known facts of history. For example, it denies that Jesus of Nazareth was crucified on a cross (Surah 4:157), something that has been substantiated, not only by the Bible, but by extrabiblical sources, such as the Jewish Talmud and Flavius Josephus.

Fourthly, the Qur'an is plagued with internal inconsistencies.[67]

Fifthly, there are no particularly good reasons to accept the Qur'an as inspired Scripture. The most popular evidence that Muslims put forth for the divine inspiration of the Qur'an is its literary beauty, but this is a highly questionable means of testing a document for divine inspiration. What would stop us from believing that Shakespeare's writings were also divinely inspired? For these reasons, and others, it is safe to conclude that the Qur'an is not divinely inspired.

ON CRUCIFIXION:

"...as a Muslim I came to believe that the crucifixion of Christ was an undisputable historical fact that no honest person that deals with evidences of history could deny."

—**Abdul Saleeb**, former Muslim, now a Christian and co-author of *Answering Islam: The Crescent in the Light of the Cross* (Baker Books; 2nd edition, 2002); online testimony: http://www.leaderu.com/wri/pages/abdul.html, 1996.

35 "What makes you think that the Book of Mormon is not trustworthy?"

First, the Book of Mormon contradicts authentic Scripture, the Bible.[68] *Secondly*, the Book of Mormon contains false prophecy.[69] *Thirdly*, it has undergone enormous change, both doctrinally and grammatically, since its initial publishing in 1830.[70] *Fourthly*, it contains extensive plagiarism of the King James Version of the Bible.[71] *Fifthly*, independent, non-Mormon archaeological verification is absolutely lacking.[72] *Sixthly*, if that was not enough, the Book of Mormon is permeated with scientific problems.[73]

For the open-minded individual who is willing to follow the evidence (or in this case, lack of evidence) wherever it leads, it is easy to see that the Book of Mormon is an early nineteenth century piece of American fiction. Orson Pratt (1811-1881), one of the early leaders in the Mormon church, said, "The Book of Mormon claims to be a divinely inspired record...*If* false [he did not think it was], it is one of the most cunning, wicked, bold, deep-laid impositions ever palmed upon the world, calculated to deceive and ruin millions."[74] The Book of Mormon *can* be proven to be false, and therefore Pratt's words stand. The Book of Mormon "is one of the most cunning, wicked, bold, deep-laid impositions ever palmed upon the world, calculated to deceive and ruin millions." I could not have said it better myself. *That* is what the Book of Mormon is.

ON THE BOOK OF MORMON:

"Archaeologists and other scholars have long probed the hemisphere's past, and the Society does not know of anything found so far that has substantiated the Book of Mormon."
–**The National Geographic Society,** August 12, 1998. View actual document at: www.irr.org/mit/natgeo.html.

"One of the most modern pretenders to inspiration is the Book of Mormon. I could not blame you should you laugh outright while I read aloud a page from that farrago."
–**Charles H. Spurgeon** (1834-1892), British preacher.

36

"If Christianity is true, why can't the different denominations agree on what to believe?"

Actually, there is great agreement amongst the different Christian denominations. When it comes to the core, foundational beliefs of Christianity, Christian churches are very unified. There *are* different opinions on some issues (e.g., what kind of worship music is best, how a local church should be governed) but when it comes to the authenticity of the Bible, the deity of Christ, what His death on the cross accomplished, His bodily resurrection from the grave, and His Second Coming, there is great harmony.

It is important to realize that disagreements

over the facts do not weaken or negate the facts. For centuries man debated and disagreed about the shape of the earth. Some said that it was round. Some thought that it was flat. During that time the earth never ceased to be round. The same is true with Christianity. The different denominations may disagree about certain aspects of church life or worship styles, but the facts stay the same. Jesus is both Lord and God and worthy of our trust and worship.

ON JESUS:

"This Jesus of Nazareth, without money and arms, conquered more millions than Alexander, Caesar, Mohammed, and Napoleon; without science and learning, He shed more light on things human and divine than all philosophers and scholars combined; without the eloquence of schools, He spoke such words of life as were never spoken before or since, and produced effects which lie beyond the reach of orator or poet; without writing a single line, He set more pens in motion, and furnished themes for more sermons, orations, discussions, learned volumes, works of art, and songs of praise than the whole army of great men of ancient and modern times."

–**Philip Schaff** (1819-1893), historian; *The Person of Christ*, 1913, pp. 29-30.

37 "Aren't there a bunch of hypocrites in the church?"

Perhaps there are. What better place for them to be? That is where they will be exposed to the Word of God and learn that hypocrisy is wrong (Matthew 23:28). Do not allow the sins of others to keep you from receiving God's free gift (Romans 6:23) of eternal life. God will deal with them. The Bible says, "each of us [which would include you] shall give account of himself to God" (Romans 14:12).

ON EVOLUTION:

"One of the reasons I started taking this anti-evolutionary view, or let's call it non-evolutionary view, was last year I had a sudden realization that for over twenty years I had thought I was working on evolution in some way. One morning I woke up and something had happened in the night and it struck me that I had been working on this stuff for twenty years and there was not one thing I knew about it. That's quite a shock to learn that one can be misled so long....For the last few weeks I've tried putting a simple question to various people and groups of people. The question is this: Can you tell me anything you know about evolution, any one thing, any one thing that you think is true? I tried that question on the geology staff at the Field Museum of Natural History and the only answer I got was silence. I tried it on the members of the Evolutionary Morphology Seminar at the University of Chicago, a very prestigious body of evolutionists, and all I got there was silence for a long time and eventually one person said, "I do know one thing—it ought not to be taught in high school."... The level of knowledge about evolution is remarkably shallow. We know it ought not to be taught in the high school and that's all we know about it."

–**Colin Patterson, Ph.D.,** former Senior Paleontologist at the British Museum of Natural History in London and editor of its journal, in a speech given at the American Museum of Natural History, New York, November 5, 1981. *Unshakable Foundations* by Norman Geisler and Peter Bocchino, 2001, p. 167.

38

"Does it really matter *what* a person believes as long as they are sincere?"

It certainly does matter. Regarding faith in Jesus, the Bible says that, "there is salvation in no one else; for there is no other name under heaven that has been given among men, by which we must be saved" (Acts 4:12, NASB). A person cannot put their faith in the god of Mormonism, a god who (according to Joseph Smith) was once a mere man who became one of many gods, and hope that that god will save him or forgive him of his sins. That god does not exist. That god was a nineteenth century invention by Joseph Smith. Millions of sincere Muslims around the world are putting their faith in Allah, the god set forth in the

Qur'an, but how is Allah going to save them? The god described in the Qur'an does not exist.[75] No amount of sincerity in the heart of a Mormon or Muslim will raise either one of these gods into being. Sincere faith is only as useful as the object in which you put your faith. A person can sincerely put his faith in a piece of yarn tied around his ankle as he bungee jumps off of the Empire State Building. Sadly, that person is going to be dead about eight seconds after he jumps.

If a person sincerely believes in Jesus, the true and living God, who actually exists, then that person is in good hands (John 10:27-30). Sincerity is important (Joshua 24:14, John 4:24), but God desires that we sincerely put our faith in *Him*, for He alone can save a person (Hosea 13:4). The gods of Hinduism, Mormonism and Islam do not exist (Isaiah 43:10b), and therefore cannot save even the sincerest of followers.

ON FACTS:

"If Christianity was something we were making up, of course we could make it easier. But it is not. We cannot compete, in simplicity, with people who are inventing religions. How could we? We are dealing with Fact. Of course anyone can be simple if he has no facts to bother about."

–**C. S. Lewis** (1898-1963), Professor of Medieval and Renaissance Literature at the University of Cambridge; *Mere Christianity*, 1943, p. 145.

39

"How could I ever be happy in heaven, knowing that my loved ones are in hell?"

It is hard to imagine being happy without our loved ones. Maybe one of the reasons God has caused us to cross paths is so that you might receive of His grace and mercy and become the instrument He uses to reach your loved ones. He does not desire that any go to hell (Ezekiel 33:11). The Bible says that God is "not willing that any should perish but that all should come to repentance" (2 Peter 3:9). He is looking for someone that He can use to help reach them (cf. Isaiah 6:8, Ezekiel 22:30).

My friend, even if your loved ones reject everything you would tell them, and end up in hell, God promises us that in His presence there is "fullness of joy" (Psalm 16:11). He also says that He is going to wipe away every tear from our eyes; and there shall no longer be *any* mourning, or crying, or pain (Revelation 21:4).

If you are concerned about your loved ones who may not go to heaven, the most irrational thing you could do is pass up God's offer of forgiveness and not go there yourself. Turn from your sins, put your faith in Christ, and allow Him to use you to reach out to them and others with the gospel.

ON FINDING GOD:

"God lets Himself be known, for example, in the story and person of Jesus. He is available to those who really want Him. "When you search for Me," the old prophet said, "you will find Me; if you seek Me with all your heart" (Jeremiah 29:13). But He will not force Himself upon you, not jump down your throat. And if you in your heart really want to be God yourself, you probably will not find Him. You will find yourself."

–Dallas Willard, Ph.D. (1935-), Professor of Philosophy at the University of Southern California, speaker, author; "The Craftiness of Christ," 2004, at http://www.dwillard.org/articles/artview. asp?artID=101.

40 "Isn't being a good person enough to get to heaven?"

That is certainly a popular belief today. From man's perspective, a person might appear to be a good person, but to God, who sees into the human heart,[76] we are all unrighteous. Jesus, Himself, said, "No one is good but One, that is, God" (Luke 18:19). Romans 3:10 says, "There is *none* righteous, no, not one." Isaiah 53:6 says, "*All* we like sheep have gone astray; we have turned, *every one*, to his own way." Obviously some people are not as evil as they could be, and some are worse than others. The bottom line is this; we all need the grace and forgiveness God offers if we are to escape the judgment we deserve and go to heaven.

Two thousand years ago, God, out of His great love for you and me, came to earth as a man and died on a cruel Roman cross. There on the cross, He took upon Himself the punishment and judgment that was due sinners (Isaiah 53:5). He rose from the grave three days later and is now graciously offering forgiveness and everlasting life (John 3:16) to all who will acknowledge their sinfulness (1 John 1:8-10), turn from their sins (Acts 17:30), and put their faith in Jesus Christ as their Lord and Savior (Romans 10:9-10). If you do that, you will be saved (Acts 16:31). The Bible says, if you go on sinning willfully after receiving the knowledge of the truth, "There will be nothing to look forward to but the terrible expectation of God's judgment and the raging fire that will consume his enemies" (Hebrews 10:27, NLT). The best decision you could ever make is to turn to Jesus, even right now, before it is too late.

ON SALVATION:

"....we have believed in Christ Jesus, that we might be accepted by God because of our faith in Christ—and not because we have obeyed the law. For no one will ever be saved by obeying the law....For if we could be saved by keeping the law, then there was no need for Christ to die."

–Paul, the apostle; Galatians 2:16b, 21b (NLT)

STEPS TO PEACE WITH GOD

1. Acknowledge that you are a sinner.

The Bible says that all of us have broken God's commandments. "There is *none* righteous, no not one....*all* have sinned" (Romans 3:10, 23). "If we say that we have no sin, we deceive ourselves" (1 John 1:8).

2. Believe that Jesus Christ died on the cross for you.

The Bible says, "If you confess with your mouth Jesus as Lord, and *believe* in your heart that God raised Him from the dead, you shall be saved" (Romans 10:9, NASB). Jesus said, "For God so loved the world that He gave His only begotten Son, that whoever *believes* in Him should not perish but have everlasting life" (John 3:16).

3. Change direction. Turn away from your sinful way of life.

The Bible says, "God is now declaring to men that

all people everywhere should repent [*repent* means to change direction, i.e., turn away from your sins], because He has fixed a day in which He will judge the world in righteousness" (Acts 17:30-31, NASB). If you are willing to repent, God will begin to change you and help you live a life that is pleasing to Him.

You can have your sins forgiven right now and begin experiencing a relationship with God today. Pray something like this:

> **"God, I confess that I am a sinner. I realize that I need Your forgiveness. I believe that You, Jesus, paid the price for my sins on the cross. I believe that You rose again from the dead and want to have a relationship with me. Thank You. Come into my life. Forgive me. Be my Lord. Be my God. I want to turn away from my sins and begin to follow You. Change me. Empower me with Your Holy Spirit to live my life for You. Amen."**

If you prayed that prayer with a sincere heart, you have begun a relationship with Jesus Christ, and God has forgiven you of your sins.

I encourage you to...

A. Begin reading and obeying the Bible. Try starting out with the Gospel of Luke in the New Testament, and follow that up by reading the Book of Acts.

B. Begin praying. Simply put, talk to God. He loves you and wants to have a relationship with you.

C. Begin going to a church that teaches through the Bible, and where the people love to worship the Lord. If they have a new believer's class, sign up to attend.

D. Make friends with other believers who can encourage you and be a blessing to you in your new relationship with Jesus. If you have a friend or a family member who is a Christian, call them and let them know of the decision you have made.

$\mathcal{A}$DDITIONAL HELP

Could you suggest any additional books for a person who wants to learn more about the evidences for the Christian faith?

Yes. There are numerous great books on Christian apologetics. Here are a few I recommend:

1. *I Don't Have Enough Faith To Be An Atheist*
   by Dr. Norman Geisler and Frank Turek

2. *The Case for Faith*
   by Lee Strobel

3. *The Case for Christ*
   by Lee Strobel

4. *The New Evidence That Demands A Verdict*
   by Dr. Josh McDowell

For additional book recommendations, articles, DVDs, CDs and other resources that will strengthen your faith, go to www.AlwaysBeReady.com

ENDNOTES

1. In 2002, the Southern Baptist Council on Family Life reported that eighty-eight percent of children raised in evangelical homes leave church at the age of eighteen, never to return. Cited at www.pastors.com/RWMT/?ID=73. Accessed on October 15, 2005.

2. I have found this question ("Do you have any spiritual beliefs?") to be a much better question than asking, "Do you believe in God?" William Fay discusses this in his excellent and helpful book on evangelism, *Share Jesus Wihout Fear* (Broadman & Holman Publishers, 1999).

3. For more on the evidence for God's existence, go to the link THE EXISTENCE OF GOD at AlwaysBeReady.com.

4. For example, consider some of the Old Testament prophecies made regarding the Messiah, whom the Old Testament prophets said would come. They prophesied hundreds of years in advance that: He would be born of the seed of Abraham (Genesis 12:1-3, 22:18), of the tribe of Judah (Genesis 49:10), of the house of David (2 Samuel 7:12f), in the city of Bethlehem (Micah 5:2), that He would come while the temple was still standing (Malachi 3:1), that He would be born of a virgin (Isaiah 7:14), that He would perform miracles (Isaiah 35:5-6), that He would be rejected by His own people (Psalm 118:22; compare with 1 Peter 2:7), that He would die at a precise time in history (Daniel 9:24-26; 483 years after the declaration to reconstruct the city of Jerusalem in 444 B.C.), how He would die (Psalm 22:16-18, Isaiah 53; Zechariah 12:10), and that He would rise from the dead (Psalm 16:10; compare with Acts 2:27-32). All of these prophecies, and hundreds of others, have been literally fulfilled. For additional examples of fulfilled prophecies in the Bible see *Every Prophecy of the Bible* by John Walvoord (Cook Communications, 2004).

5. There are some verses in the Bible that *do* appear on the surface to contradict each other, but with a little investigation into the original languages, the cultural context, and the geographical settings, they are easily cleared up. See my study entitled, "An Examination of Apparent Contradictions in

the Bible," at AlwaysBeReady.com. In this study I discuss the solutions to popularly cited apparent contradictions in the Bible. To find this study click on the link BIBLE.

6. For more on the trustworthiness of the Bible, go to the link BIBLE at AlwaysBeReady.com.

7. Norman L. Geisler, *Baker Encyclopedia of Christian Apologetics* (Grand Rapids, MI: Baker, 1999), p. 187.

8. Some examples would be Tertullian, Justin Martyr, Eusebius and Polycarp.

9. An excellent book that addresses the Bible's manuscript evidence is *A General Introduction to the Bible* by Norman Geisler and William Nix, (Moody Publishers; Revised and Expanded edition, 1986). I have also written a brief article on this topic. Go to the link BIBLE at AlwaysBeReady.com.

10. See Acts 10, where Peter is sent to Cornelius.

11. For example, see Daniel 2, where Nebuchadnezzar is given a vision. Norman Geisler and Ron Rhodes, *When Cultists Ask*, (Grand Rapids, MI: Baker Books, 1997), p. 209.

12. For more help answering objections to the

Bible's teaching on hell, go to the link HELL at AlwaysBeReady.com.

13. Lee Strobel, *The Case for Christ* (Grand Rapids, Mich.: Zondervan, 1998), p. 260.

14. Flavius Josephus, *The Antiquities of the Jews*, 18:63-64 (Hendrickson Publishers, 1987; eighteenth printing), p. 480.

15. *The Babylonian Talmud: Tractate Sanhedrin,* Folio 43a, 33-34.

16. See John 19:14, Luke 22:15.

17. An excellent book on the evidence for Jesus' life is *The Historical Jesus: Ancient Evidence for the Life of Christ* by Gary Habermas (College Press, 1996). Even as we are about to take this book, *One Minute Answers To Skeptics' Top Forty Questions,* to press, a story has just come out of Israel concerning fresh, new evidence regarding Jesus. The Foxnews.com headline (November 8, 2005) read, "Israel Church a Major Discovery." Here is an excerpt from their report: "Israeli prisoner Ramil Razilo was removing rubble from the planned site of a new prison ward when his shovel uncovered the edge of an elaborate mosaic, unveiling what Israeli archaeologists said Sunday may be the Holy Land's oldest church. The discovery of the church in the northern Israeli town of Megiddo,

near the biblical Armageddon, was hailed by experts as an important discovery that could reveal details about the development of the early church in the region. Archaeologists said the church dated from the third century, decades before Constantine legalized Christianity across the Roman Empire....Channel Two television, which first reported the story, broadcast pictures of a detailed and well-preserved mosaic bearing the name of Jesus Christ in ancient Greek and images of fish." (I accessed this Foxnews.com story on November 15, 2005). CNN.com reported, "Two mosaics inside the church–one covered with fish, an ancient Christian symbol that predates the cross–tell the story of a Roman officer and a woman named Aketous who donated money to build the church in the memory "of the god, Jesus Christ." (CNN.com story accessed November 15, 2005). This discovery not only affirms that Jesus lived, but it also helps to verify that the early church believed He was God.

18. Jesus said, "I am the way, the truth, and the life. No one comes to the Father except through Me" (John 14:6). Regarding faith in Jesus, Peter said, "there is salvation in no one else; for there is no other name under heaven that has been given among men, by which we must be saved" (Acts 4:12, NASB). Also see: 1 Timothy 2:5, Matthew 7:13, and Isaiah 43:11.

19. An examination of some of the Ten Commandments is all that is necessary to realize that Romans 3:10 is

true when it states, "There is *none* righteous, no, not one." In Exodus 20, God states, "You shall have no other gods before Me....You shall not take the name of the LORD your God in vain, for the LORD will not hold him guiltless who takes His name in vain.... Honor your father and your mother....You shall not murder. You shall not commit adultery. You shall not steal. You shall not bear false witness against your neighbor. You shall not covet your neighbor's house; you shall not covet your neighbor's wife,...nor anything that is your neighbor's."

20. This is something that Dan Brown says occurred in his popular, yet highly inaccurate novel, *The Da Vinci Code* (Doubleday, 2003), p. 233. For a response to many of the book's erroneous claims, go to the link DA VINCI CODE at AlwaysBeReady.com.

21. For more help defending the Bible's teaching regarding the deity of Christ, go to the link DEITY OF CHRIST at AlwaysBeReady.com.

22. Ignatius (A.D. 30-98 or 107), the Bishop of Antioch, referred to Jesus with words like: "Jesus Christ our God," "Jesus...who is God and man," "Suffer me to follow the example of the passion of my God," "Our God Jesus Christ," "There is One God who manifests himself through Jesus Christ his son," "God Incarnate." Dr. Erwin Lutzer points out that the fact that Ignatius was not rebuked, nor branded as a

heretic by any of the churches or Christian leaders he sent such letters to, proves that the early church, long before the Council of Nicea in 325 A.D., believed that Jesus was God. Justin Martyr (A.D. 100-165) said of Jesus: "...being the first-begotten Word of God, is even God," "...both God and Lord of hosts." Irenaeus (A.D. 120-202) said, "...our Lord, and God, and Savior, and King." Clement of Alexandria (A.D. 150-215) said of Jesus: "...truly most manifest Deity, He that is made equal to the Lord of the universe; because he was His Son."

23. *The Problem of Pain*, by C. S. Lewis (1898-1963), included in *The Quotable Lewis* (Tyndale, 1989).

24. This last sentence is a paraphrase of J. P. Moreland's comments in Lee Strobel's interview of him in *The Case for Faith* (Grand Rapids, Mich.: Zondervan, 2000), p. 178.

25. For example, consider these demeaning words that the Gospel of Thomas puts in the mouths of the apostle Peter and Jesus in verse 114. Peter supposedly says, "Make Mary leave us, for females don't deserve life." Jesus said, "Look, I will guide her to make her male, so that she too may become a living spirit resembling you males. For every female who makes herself male will enter the domain of Heaven." Sayings like these made it obvious to the early Christians that these Gnostic gospels were not

authentic, divinely inspired Scripture.

26. By *Apocrypha* I am referring to fourteen Jewish writings, written between 200 B.C. and A.D. 100, in between the completion of the Old Testament and before the establishment of the New Testament. Today, eleven of those books (e.g., Tobit, Judith, First and Second Maccabees, Baruch) are accepted by the Catholic Church as God-inspired Scripture and are even placed in the Catholic Bible.

27. For more information on the Apocrypha, go to the link ROMAN CATHOLICISM at AlwaysBeReady. com.

28. For example, in the Book of Judith (1:1) we are told that Nebuchadnezzar reigned in the city of Nineveh. It is a widely known historical fact that this was never the case. Nebuchadnezzar was the king of Babylonia in Babylon. Elsewhere, in the Apocrypha, we are told that Tobit was alive when the Assyrians conquered Israel in 722 B.C. and also when Jeroboam revolted against Judah in 931 B.C., which would make him at least 209 years old; yet according to the account (Tobit 14:11), he died when he was 158 years.

29. In the New Testament book of Jude (vs. 9, 14-15), there are some allusions to extra-biblical writings such as, the *Book of Enoch* (v. 14-15) and the *Bodily Assumption of Moses*. Keep in mind that Jude does

not cite these books as being inspired Scripture or divinely authoritative. He simply refers to a truth contained in those books which otherwise may have many errors. I mention this to make clear that these citations do not lend any support to the Catholic position, for even the Roman Catholic Church rejects those two particular books as non-canonical.

30. I would recommend that every student of the Bible own the book *When Critics Ask*, by Dr. Norman Geisler and Thomas Howe (Baker Books, 1992). It is an excellent handbook on Bible difficulties. Make sure to read the introduction, where Geisler and Howe examine seventeen mistakes critics make when interpreting the Bible. Two other excellent resources are the *New International Encyclopedia of Bible Difficulties* by Gleason Archer (Zondervan; Reprint edition, 2001) and *Hard Sayings of the Bible* by Walter Kaiser, Peter Davids, F.F. Bruce and Manfred Brauch (Intervarsity Press, 1996). There are also many apologetics websites that address apparent contradictions. For instance, see carm.org and christiananswers.net.

31. Even the liberal scholar, John A. T. Robinson, concedes in his book, *Redating the New Testament* (Westminster Press, 1976), that past scholarship suggesting a late completion date for the New Testament was based on a "tyranny of unexamined assumptions" and an "almost willful blindness" on the

part of the critics. Robinson concluded that the entire New Testament was written before the destruction of the temple in A.D. 70. I would largely agree with him on this matter, except to say that there *is* good evidence, in the writings of the church fathers, that the Book of Revelation was written near the end of Domitian's reign, around A.D. 95.

32. For more on the dating of the New Testament go to the link BIBLE at AlwaysBeReady.com and see the article, "When Was the New Testament Completed?"

33. See the Qur'an, Surah 19:30-35.

34. Regarding this popular notion that Jesus was only "a good teacher," C. S. Lewis said, "I am trying here to prevent anyone saying the really foolish thing that people often say about Him: 'I'm ready to accept Jesus as a great moral teacher, but I don't accept His claim to be God.' That is the one thing we must not say. A man who was merely a man and said the sort of things Jesus said would not be a great moral teacher. He would either be a lunatic–on the level with the man who says he is a poached egg–or else he would be the Devil of Hell. You must make your choice. Either this man was, and is, the Son of God: or else a madman or something worse. You can shut Him up for a fool, you can spit at Him and kill Him as a demon; or you can fall at His feet and call Him Lord and God. But let us not come with any patronizing nonsense about

His being a great human teacher. He has not left that open to us. He did not intend to." (*Mere Christianity*, The MacMillan Company, 1960, pp. 40-41).

35. Luke 24:25-27, John 5:46, Acts 3:18. For a partial list of Old Testament prophecies that were fulfilled in the life of Christ, see www.christiananswers.net/dictionary/messianic prophecies.html.

36. Hebrews 4:15, John 8:46.

37. John 10:36-38, Mark 2:10-12.

38. Romans 1:4, John 2:18-22.

39. According to Buddhist tradition, it was Buddha's imperfections that required him to live more than a hundred thousand past lives working off his karma and building up the perfections that he needed to finally become a Buddha like others who had achieved that state before him. Concerning Muhammad, we are told that he cried out, "O Allah! Set me apart from my sins (faults) as the East and West are set apart from each other and clean me from sins as a white garment is cleaned of dirt (after thorough washing). O Allah! Wash off my sins with water, snow and hail" (*The Hadith*, Volume 1, Book 12, Number 711, narrated Abu Huraira). In addition to the Hadith, the Qur'an also identifies Muhammad as a sinner. See Surah 40:55, 48:2, and 47:19.

40. Some of the evidences for Christ's resurrection are discussed in question 19.

41. When I talk to a person who has chosen a homosexual lifestyle, I rarely even bring up their sexual preference. I use God's law, the Ten Commandments, when witnessing to a homosexual. The Bible tells us that the law was made for homosexuals. 1 Timothy 1:8-11 says, "But we know that the law is good if one uses it lawfully, knowing this: that the law is not made for a righteous person, but for [who is it made for?] the lawless and insubordinate, for the ungodly and for sinners, for the unholy and profane, for murderers of fathers and murderers of mothers, for manslayers, for fornicators, for sodomites [The NASB translates this word as "homosexuals"], for kidnappers, for liars, for perjurers, and if there is any other thing that is contrary to sound doctrine, according to the glorious gospel of the blessed God which was committed to my trust." If you use the law when you witness to a homosexual you will not even have to touch on their sexual preference, and therefore be accused of hating homosexuals. The law will show the homosexual that he is guilty of numerous other sins. When the homosexual turns to God, puts his faith in Jesus, and is born again, God will give him a new heart with new desires (Ezekiel 36:25-27, 2 Corinthians 5:17, Ephesians 4:22-24). This approach with homosexuals is something I gleaned from Ray

Comfort (see his website at www.livingwaters.com).

42. Stephen (Acts 7:59-60) was the first of many of the early church's martyrs. See *Foxe's Book of Martyrs* by John Foxe (1516-1587) to read how the original disciples and others, like John Hus, John Wycliffe and William Tyndale, were persecuted and killed. This book can be read online at http://xweb1. calvarychapel.com/php/ccmain/library/bom.php.

43. I suggest that you be prepared to tell the person about some of the amazing ways God has worked in your own life.

44. For a long list of Ph. D. holding scientists from Yale, Princeton, Stanford, MIT, UC Berkeley, UCLA, and other prestigious institutions, who are skeptical of the Darwinian theory of evoltion, see www. dissentfromdarwin.org.

45. For an excellent treatment of this topic see Michael Behe's book *Darwin's Black Box* (The Free Press, 1996).

46. Carl Sagan. "Life" in *Encyclopedia Britannica: Macropaedia* (1974 ed.), pp. 893-894.

47. A former Darwinist posted these comments on Amazon.com after reading *Icons of Evolution*, "I must admit that reading this book was somewhat shocking. I had expected to see rehashed creationist

arguments about the Second Law of Thermodynamics and the lack of transitional forms in the fossil
record. On the contrary, nothing Wells says depends
on creationist ideas. He has collected evidence from
the mainstream, peer-reviewed scientific literature,
and combined them into a compelling case against
what we might call "textbook Darwinism." This
might be a trivial accomplishment, since the record
of high school and college textbooks is generally
dismal. But his cumulative argument seems to me
devastating to orthodox Neo-Darwinism, since it just
is textbook Darwinism. Wells discusses the famous
comparative vertebrate embryo diagrams—which
should be an embarrassment to any textbook author
who includes them—the fallacious way homology is
used for evidence of common ancestry, the collapse
of the story of Peppered Moths, Darwin's finches, and
many more pieces of the Darwinist lore. By the time
I was finished, I had lost faith in almost everything I
thought I knew about evolution. I now suspect that
Darwin will soon join company with Marx and Freud.
I'm not sure what I believe at this point, but I can
no longer buy the official story." (Comments posted
on November 22, 2000 and accessed on October 9,
2005).

48. David Hume to John Stewart, February, 1754, in
The Letters of David Hume, ed. J. Y. T. Greig (Oxford:
Clarendon Press, 1932), 1:187.

49. For more on this topic of God's existence, go to the link THE EVIDENCE FOR GOD'S EXISTENCE at AlwaysBeReady.com.

50. When we speak of God being omnipotent, or all-powerful, we are affirming that God can do whatever is possible to do. It is impossible for God to do things contrary to His unchanging nature. For example, God "cannot lie" (Titus 1:2), "God cannot be tempted by evil" (James 1:13), or cease to exist (Pslam 90:2).

51. Here is the dilemma. Genesis chapter four says that Adam and Eve had three boys, Cain, Abel and Seth. Then it says in Genesis 4:17 that Cain knew his wife and she conceived a child named Enoch. "Well," the skeptic says, "If Adam and Eve were the first people God made, where in the world did Cain get his wife?"

52. Support for the 1446 B.C. date of the Exodus from Egypt, followed shortly by the giving of the law to Moses, "comes from the biblical record and archeological evidence. First, in 1 Kings 6:1 the time between the Exodus and the beginning of Solomon's temple construction (in the fourth year of his reign) was 480 years. Since the fourth year of Solomon's reign was 966 B.C., the Exodus was in 1446. Also in the time of Jephthah (ca. 1100 B.C.) Israel had been in the land for 300 years (Judges 11:26). Therefore 300 years plus the 40 years of the wilderness sojourn

and some time to conquer Heshbon places the Exodus in the middle of the 15th century." (*Bible Knowledge Commentary/Old Testament* © 1983, 2000 Cook Communications Ministries).

53. Jim Tetlow writes, "To marry near of kin in the ancient world was common. Yet, beginning about 1500 B.C., God forbid this practice. The reason is simple– the genetic mutations (resulting from the curse) had a cumulative effect. Though Cain could safely marry his sister because the genetic pool was still relatively pure at that time, by Moses' day the genetic errors had swelled. Today, geneticists confirm that the risk of passing on a genetic abnormality to your child is much greater if you marry a close relative because relatives are more likely to carry the same defective gene. If they procreate, their offspring are more apt to have this defect expressed." (*101 Scientific Facts and Foreknowledge,* Eternal Productions, 2005, number 48).

54. See 1 Peter 3:15 and 2 Timothy 2:24-26.

55. See a photograph of a petroglyph of a sauropod dinosaur in *The Revised and Expanded Answers Book*, edited by Don Batten, Ph.D., Ken Ham, Jonathan Sarfati and Carl Wieland (Master Books, 2000; Reprinted August 2003), p. 246. You may also view a couple of these petroglyphs online at: www.rae.org/dinoglyph.html

56. Some accounts say 1841, others say 1842. *The Encyclopedia Britannica* says, "Before Richard Owen introduced the term *Dinosauria* in 1842, there was no concept of anything even like a dinosaur." (From "Dinosaur" entry on Encyclopedia Britannica 2004 Ultimate Reference Suite DVD).

57. See http://teacher.scholastic.com/researchtools/articlearchives/dinos/dinobaby.htm. Accessed on October 11, 2005.

58. "Although there are about 668 names of dinosaurs, there are perhaps only 55 different "kinds" of dinosaurs" (www.answersingenesis.org/docs2/4351news7-26-2000.asp). Accessed on October 11, 2005.

59. "According to Genesis 6:15, the Ark measured 300 x 50 x 30 cubits, which is about 460 x 75 x 44 feet, with a volume of 1.54 million cubic feet. Researchers have shown that this is the equivalent volume of 522 standard railroad stock cars (US), each of which can hold 240 sheep. By the way, only 11% of all land animals are larger than a sheep." (www.answersingenesis.org/docs2/4351news7-26-2000.asp). Accessed on October 11, 2005. For a thoroughly researched book that answers just about every conceivable question or attack on the feasibility of Noah's Ark, I highly recommend John

Woodmorappe's book *Noah's Ark: A Feasibility Study* (Institute for Creation Research, 1996).

60. Henry M. Morris, *Science and the Bible, Revised and Expanded* (Chicago, Moody Press, 1986), p.77.

61. I drew much of my answer for this question from information provided by Answers In Genesis. See their website at www.answersingenesis.org.

62. See Surahs 112:1-4 and 4:48 in the Qur'an.

63. For example, Surah 2:276 says, "Allah does not love any ungrateful sinner." Surah 3:32 says, "surely Allah does not love the unbelievers." Surah 4:36 says, "surely Allah does not love him who is proud." Surah 6:141 says, "surely He does not love the extravagant."

64. See *Unveiling Islam* (Kregel Publications, 2002) by Ergun and Emir Caner, two former Muslims who are now committed Christians, for a great insider's look at Muslim life and beliefs.

65. For a more in-depth look at Islam, go to the link ISLAM at AlwaysBeReady.com. The book *Answering Islam: The Crescent in Light of the Cross* (Baker Books; Second edition, 2002), by Norman Geisler and Abdul Saleeb (a former Muslim, now a Christian), is also an excellent resource.

66. The Bible spoke accurately about the sun some 1,500 years before Muhammad was born, saying of the sun, "Its rising is from one end of *heaven*, and its circuit to the other end" (Psalm 19:6).

67. Here are just a couple of examples. The Qur'an teaches that Noah and all of his family survived the Flood in one place (Surah 21:76), but in another place it states that one of Noah's sons drowned (Surah 11:42-43). The Qur'an states that Pharaoh drowned (Surah 28:40 and others 17:103, 43:55) but in another place it says that he survived (Surah 10:90-92). For more examples of contradictions in the Qur'an, see http://answering-islam.org/Quran/Contra.

68. Here are four examples. The Bible says there was darkness for three *hours* while Jesus was on the cross (Matthew 27:45; Mark 15:33; Luke 23:44). According to a Book of Mormon prophecy (Helaman 14:27), at the time of Christ's crucifixion "darkness should cover the face of the whole earth for the space of three *days*." The Bible says that Jesus was born in the town of Bethlehem (Luke 2:4, Micah 5:2). According to the Book of Mormon, Jesus was born in Jerusalem (Alma 7:10). The Bible says believers were first called Christians after Paul's ministry in Antioch (Acts 11:26). The Book of Mormon claims people were known by this title as early as 73 B.C. (Alma 46:15). In the Old Testament the only ones who could be priests were the descendants of Levi,

one of the twelve sons of Israel (Numbers 3:9-10). The Book of Mormon claims that descendants of the tribe of Manasseh were made priests (Alma 10:3, 2 Nephi 5:26). The Book of Mormon has many of these kinds of contradictions. For more examples see http:// www.irr.org/mit/bombible.html and www.utlm.org.

69. Speaking of the Jews, the Book of Mormon prophesies in 2 Nephi 10:7, "But behold, thus saith the Lord *God*: When the day cometh that they shall believe in me, that I am *Christ*, then have I covenanted with their fathers that they shall be restored in the flesh, upon the earth, unto the lands of their inheritance." According to the Book of Mormon, God prophesies that the Jews would be restored to their land, but only when they would acknowledge Jesus as God. Well, the Jews are back in their land today, but who would suggest that it happened as a result of their having believed that Jesus was God? That certainly was not the case. According to the Deuteronomy 18:20-22, God's prophets had to be correct 100% of the time. The Book of Mormon has failed the test. Joseph Smith made other false prophecies. See: http://www. utlm.org/onlineresources/falseprophecies.htm.

70. Joseph Smith himself said that the golden plates, from which he supposedly got the Book of Mormon, were translated letter-by-letter, and "by the power of God" (*History of the Church*, i, p. 54-55) and that the Book of Mormon was "the most correct of any book

on earth" (*History of the Church*, 4:461; this is also stated in the Introduction of the Book of Mormon). If that were true, there should not have been a need for any corrections–*even* spelling and grammatical errors. But, there *have* been changes. Lots of them. In fact, there have been more than 4,000 changes made to the Book of Mormon between the time that the original was published in 1830 and current edition published in 1981 (Ron Rhodes and Marian Bodine, *Reasoning from The Scriptures With The Mormons*, 1995, p. 117). Many of the changes were corrections to Joseph Smith's misspellings and grammatical errors, but there have been many more changes that are quite substantial. One example can be seen in 1 Nephi 11:21 where it says (in the 1830 edition) that Jesus is "the eternal *Father*." Today's version says (in the same verse) that Jesus is: "the *son* of the eternal Father." Go to http://www.utlm.org/onlinebooks/ 3913intro.htm to see numerous other examples. To see scanned pages of the original 1830 version of the Book of Mormon go to http://www.irr.org/mit/BOM/ 1830bom-books.html.

71. As you know, to plagiarize is to take ideas, or writings, from another and offer them as one's own. The Book of Mormon does this hundreds of times. It puts forth some 27,000 words, verses and paragraphs that were taken directly from the King James Version of the Bible (Ron Rhodes and Marian Bodine, *Reasoning from The Scriptures With The Mormons*,

1995, p. 121). There are even whole chapters lifted right out of the King James Version. In fact, even the *italicized* words in the King James Version have been plagiarized. The italicized words, as noted in the preface of the King James Version, were added by the King James translators to add clarity. And yet, even those words ended up in the Book of Mormon! If, as Joseph Smith says, the golden plates he supposedly translated, were originally penned between 600 B.C. and A.D. 421, how could the Book of Mormon contain such extensive quotations from the King James Version of the Bible, that was written in Old English, and wasn't even published until 1611 (over a 1,000 years later)? That is a question the Mormon Church does not like to be asked.

72. The Book of Mormon tells us of two different nations that supposedly once existed in North America: the Nephite and Lamanite nations. We are told in the Book of Mormon that these nations had huge populations who lived in large, fortified cities. They allegedly waged large-scale wars with each other for hundreds of years in which hundreds of thousands of people were killed. The final battle was in A.D. 385 near Hill Cumorah in present-day New York State (see Mormon 6:9-15 in the Book of Mormon). Yet despite these huge populations, cities, and wars, archaeologists have not been able to discover a single thing that would indicate that these people groups ever existed, or that these events

actually ever occurred. Dave Hunt writes, "Not one piece of evidence has ever been found to support the Book of Mormon–not a trace of the large cities it names, no ruins, no coins, no letters or documents or monuments, nothing in writing. Not even one of the rivers or mountains or any of the topography it mentions has ever been identified" (*In Defense of the Faith,* Harvest House, 1996, p. 156). This has been verified by the Smithsonian Institute in Washington D.C. which stated in 1980, "The Smithsonian Institution has never used The Book of Mormon in any way as a scientific guide. Smithsonian archaeologists see *no direct connection* between the archaeology of the New World and the subject matter of the book." *National Geographic* magazine stated in 1990 that, "...there is *no* archaeological evidence to verify the history of early peoples of the Western Hemisphere as presented in the Book of Mormon." On August 12, 1998, the National Geographic Society stated, "Archaeologists and other scholars have long probed the hemisphere's past, and the Society does not know of anything found so far that has substantiated the Book of Mormon." If a Mormon tells you that archaeological evidence *does* exist, put the burden of proof on them. Ask for documentation from non-Mormon sources that you can examine.

73. Dr. Thomas Key, Ph.D., Sc.D., Ed.D. has written a book, *The Book of Mormon in the Light of Science* (Utah Missions, Inc.; Revised Edition, 2004), in

which he documents numerous problems in the Book of Mormon. Among the problems he cites are the Book of Mormon's: archaeological problems, astronomical problems, botanical problems, chemical problems, geographical problems, geological problems, historical problems, linguistics problems, mathematical problems, microbiological problems, physics problems, and zoological problems. You can download a free copy of this book at http://tdkey.com.

74. Orson Pratt's Works, "Divine Authenticity of the Book of Mormon" (Liverpool, 1851), pp. 1-2.

75. See questions 33 and 34 that also address issues related to Islam.

76. 1 Samuel 16:7 says, "man looks at the outward appearance, but the LORD looks at the heart."

ABOUT THE AUTHOR

 Charlie H. Campbell has been a pastor at Calvary Chapel Vista in southern California since 1997. He is the Director of the Always Be Ready Apologetics Ministry and a frequent guest speaker at churches around the United States. He is also the Director of The School of Ministry at Calvary Chapel Vista where he teaches courses on apologetics, world religions, cults, Bible prophecy, preaching, hermeneutics, systematic theology, and evangelism.

BOOKING INFORMATION

If you would like to inquire about having Charlie Campbell teach at your church, youth group, camp, conference, or school, please email: info @AlwaysBeReady.com or visit: www.AlwaysBe Ready.com and click CONTACT.

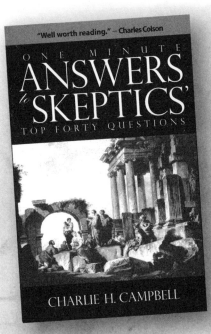
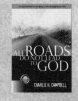